D0601236

Beautiful Bedrooms

AROUND THE WORLD

Beautiful
Bedrooms

AROUND THE WORLD

PHOTOGRAPHS BY DEIDI VON SCHAEWEN ✺ TEXT BY FRANCESCA TORRE

Stewart, Tabori & Chang
New York

Published in 2008 by Stewart, Tabori & Chang
An imprint of Harry N. Abrams, Inc.

Copyright © 2007 by Aubanel, an imprint of Editions Minerva, Geneva,
Switzerland
English translation copyright © 2008 by Stewart, Tabori & Chang, New York

Library of Congress Cataloging-in-Publication Data
Torre, Francesca.
 Beautiful bedrooms around the world / by Francesca Torre ; photographs by
 Deidi von Schaewen.
 p. cm.
 ISBN 978-1-58479-725-8
 1. Bedrooms. 2. Interior decoration. I. Schaewen, Deidi von, 1941- II.
 Title.
 NK2117.B4T67 2008
 747.7'7—dc22
 2008004007

Design: Catherine Barluet & Julie Lecœur (lecoeurbarluet.com)
Editor: Laure Lamendin
Copyeditor: Jean Bernard-Maugiron & Armelle Heron

Translated from the French by Krister Swartz
Editor, English-language edition: Miranda Ottewell
Designer, English-language edition: Shawn Dahl
Production Manager, English-language edition: Jules Thomson

The text of this book was composed in Proxima Nova, Nobel and Miller.

Printed and bound in China
10 9 8 7 6 5 4 3 2 1

HNA
harry n. abrams, inc.
a subsidiary of La Martinière Groupe

115 West 18th Street
New York, NY 10011
www.hnabooks.com

CONTENTS

FOREWORD

From a single animal pet on the ground, through the communal sleeping hall of medieval castles, to the grandeur of Louis XIV's suite, humans have always sought out comfort and warmth to help them cope with the vulnerability of sleep. We have always sought the intimacy of a cave, room, alcove, boudoir, or four-poster bed to shield us from cold and drafts, from heat or light, and to protect our defenseless sleeping bodies from the dangers of the world outside. The history of the bedroom, the kingdom of dreams, rest, sleep, and love, is fascinating. Even more so is the evolution of the bed and the central position it has occupied in social life through the ages.

From ancient Rome—"the civilization of the bed," where people not only slept but dined, read, and entertained while reclining—to the Middle Ages, when beds could be dismantled and moved out of the way in the daytime, or taken along on travels; from beds equipped with curtains that could be rolled up during the day and let down again at night to beds of state where royalty might give audience to visitors, this history has left its mark on the decoration of present-day bedrooms.

This book assembles some of the most exceptional examples of bedrooms from every corner of the globe. Originality, luxury, innovation, and above all, absolute freedom characterize these bedrooms, which, though sometimes unusual, always arouse the senses. Designer bedrooms, contemporary or classical; bedrooms inspired by the Orient, Asia, or Africa; designers' or artists' extravagant flights of fancy; even sleeping rooms open to the sky—each represents not only its own unique decor, but its creator's way of life and attitude toward sleep.

Inveterate traveler and design photographer of international renown Deidi von Schaewen crisscrossed the planet—from New York to New Delhi, from the Maghreb to Indonesia, from the islands of the Pacific to the deepest heart of Africa—to seek out the most beautiful interiors for this book. Not only do her photographs allow us to enter into the intimacy of a succession of bedrooms, but they also show us what inspires the dreams of these rooms' occupants—for where we sleep reveals, often despite us, our tastes, our interests, and our unique style of living. The bedroom is also the place where each of us can experiment with our urges, our fantasies, and our personality, stamping as our own this most private haven.

The bed is always the essential element—and the style and range of beds varies from one country to the next, influenced by culture as well as climate. All over the world, the way we sleep has its own style, and the bedroom is central to each culture. From the tatami mats of Japan to the carved wooden headrests of Africa, from colonial beds to hammocks, this book offers a voyage to civilizations around the world, at the same time serving as a prodigious source of inspiration. It unfolds like a fabulous history of the decorative arts, traversing the five continents.

FRANCESCA TORRE

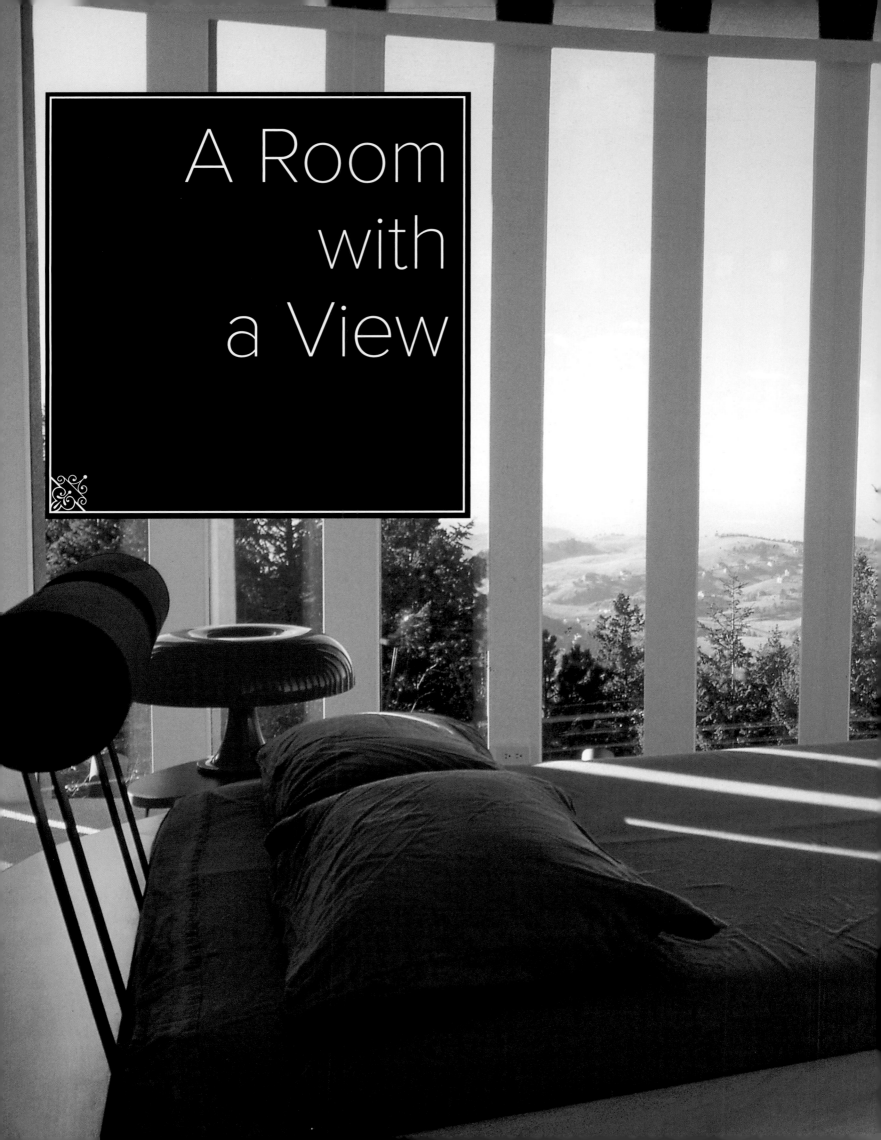

A Room with a View

The well-being of the body and the spirit is cultivated through all five senses. Among these, however, sight is often the first to reveal to us the aesthetic qualities of a place or an object. The eye is, in effect, the organ that allows us to identify that which surrounds us: shapes, distances, textures, colors, sizes, perspectives, and depths. This is why what we see in—and the view from—a bedroom affects our impression of its comfort and elegance as much as, if not more than, any other element.

Emancipated from limiting preconceptions, the inhabitants of the houses in this section are free to live and build where they choose. The main idea here is to get as much as possible out of the beauty of the site and the view through the liberal use of windows. Nothing, or next to nothing, hinders the eye as it looks out into infinity.

The residences presented in this chapter are in perfect harmony with the natural landscapes they are set in, whether rocky, severe, almost austere, or exuberant with lush tropical vegetation. In this section, we begin with the most contemporary of urban settings, and end in the magnificent landscape of the African savannah.

Those looking for something spectacular and original will not be disappointed. At first glance, we are struck by the details that make these spaces so special—the architecture, the grand spaces, picture windows offering almost 360-degree views, polished wood floors, wonderful headboards, monumental stones serving as low tables.

In Los Angeles, there is magic in being able to lie down in a room literally suspended above a megalopolis, and take in the fascinating spectacle of the city spread out before your eyes. Inside, materials such as wood, metal, glass, or concrete increase the textural and chromatic effects.

In Botswana, by the Okavango Delta, a well-designed and beautifully crafted structure is raised on stilts. Though it includes a lounge, a bath, and a bedroom, these rooms are not permanent: two of the four walls are movable, and can be opened during the day and closed at night.

In Galle, Sri Lanka, there's no reason to fear the encroachment of new buildings, since the house is set in the very middle of a palm plantation.

The houses presented in this chapter are often primary residences. In these pleasant and light-filled spaces, which welcome the outdoors inside, the inhabitants do not merely pose in contemplation. They are literally immersed in the universe that surrounds them.

PREVIOUS SPREAD, LEFT, AND OPPOSITE:

DENVER

Built in the 1960s by Charles Deaton, this sculptural and experimental house was intended to accommodate the architect and his family. It remained unfinished and unoccupied, however, for thirty-five years.

Deaton, inspired by the forms of rocks eroded by the wind, drew as well on his education as an aeronautic engineer. The Sculptured House, as he liked to call it at the end of his life, is situated 8,900 feet above sea level and offers panoramic views over Denver and the mountains. It took almost eighteen months for John J. Huggins to transform this abandoned work into a weekend residence for the architect's daughter Charlee and her husband, Nick Antonopoulos. Inside the flying saucer, movement flows easily from one space to another.

ABOVE AND OPPOSITE:

NEW YORK

In the very heart of Manhattan, the
Metropolitan Tower is a seventy-eight-floor
skyscraper of glass triangles. This bedroom
on the top floor, designed by Andrée Putman,
feels like a spacious ship's cabin, with a view
out on the city lights or the starry sky.
At the foot of the bed is a rug by Eileen
Gray, at the head are bedside tables by
Pierre Chareau. Near a telescope is Patrick
Naggar's Hell's Angel chair, a small sly wink
from the French designer.

OVERLEAF:

LOS ANGELES

The angularity of John Lautner's architecture
is echoed in the furniture chosen by the
present owner, John Goldstein. The bed faces
picture windows that, with a simple push of a
button, open onto a breathtaking panorama.

PREVIOUS SPREAD:

**LITTLE KULALA,
NAMIBIA**

Raw materials and organic
forms blend perfectly with
the untouched landscape
of the Namib Desert.

LEFT:

**LITTLE KULALA,
NAMIBIA**

At the foot of the bed,
designer Laurie Owen
has set low tables made of
large, smooth boulders on
a carpet custom-made by
hand from small strips of
leather.

OPPOSITE:

**GALLE,
SRI LANKA**

Built for the two American
writers Gordon Merrik
and Charles Hulse, and
owned today by Jean
Hassid, this house is set
deep in the heart of a palm
plantation. The omnipres-
ence of nature and the
Dutch colonial furniture
invite a wonderful
laziness. The windows
have been replaced by
screens, allowing the air to
circulate easily.

PHUKET, THAILAND

Nestled into a wall of vegetation, this bedroom and bath by Ed Tuttle are paneled in maka wood. When windows are closed, light enters the room through frosted glass like in traditional Thai houses. There is free movement from one room to the other. This residence is found on the property of the Amanpuri Hotel.

BALI

In Anneke van Waesberg's house, which is totally open to nature, a spacious balcony over-
hangs frangipani trees. A mattress and pillows in cotton covers soften the teak daybed.

UBUD, BALI

Perched high above the gorge of the Ayung River, this room in the luxury Amandari Hotel
glorifies the riches of Balinese culture. Stretched across the head and roof of the canopy bed,
tapestries evoke the history of the country.

THE OKAVANGO DELTA, BOTSWANA

At Mombo Camp, Silvio Rech and Leslie Carsten have designed the bed/sitting room around a large porch overlooking the savannah. The wooden structure is covered in cloth. The decoration subtly mixes linen, leather, ceruse wood, and African textiles with geometric patterns.

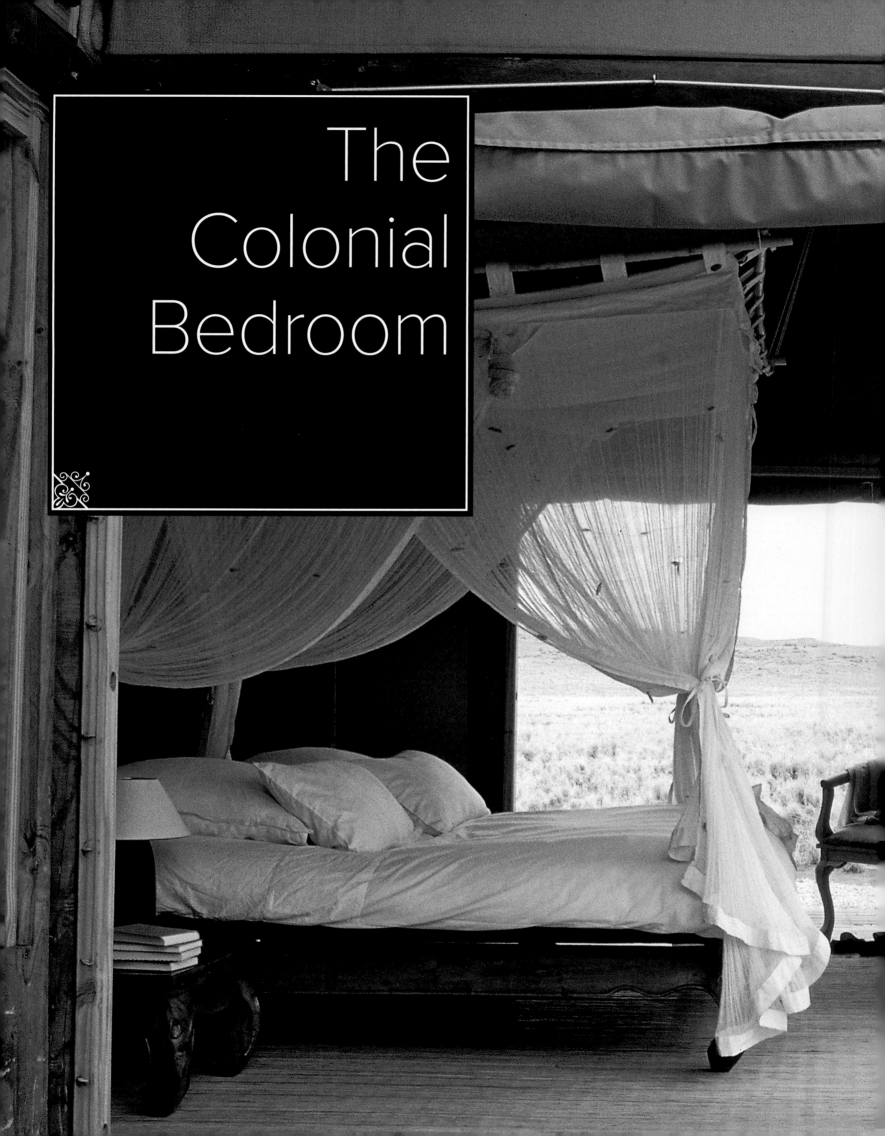

The Colonial Bedroom

The houses of the French and British colonies at their height transport us to a sophisticated universe of elegance and poetry. We are immediately struck by the sublime Africa of Karen Blixen (known to the literary world as Isak Dinesen): "Africa distilled up through six thousand feet like the strong and refined essence of a continent. . . . The views were immensely wide—everything that you saw made for greatness and freedom, and unequalled nobility." It is not hard to imagine the safaris she thrillingly brings to life: "There is something about safari life that makes you forget all of your sorrows and feel as if you had drunk half a bottle of champagne—bubbling over with heartfelt gratitude for being alive." Her African farmhouse, like all colonial buildings, was conceived to keep its occupants—people who were drawn to a climate without winter, but confronted by great heat and abundant tropical rains—dry and cool.

In these exquisitely cool residences, a great variety of exotic woods are used: massive beams supporting roofs, verandas ornamented with friezes, and large shutter panels filter the sun and the breeze. The bedrooms often have electric fans and four-poster beds with silky muslin. Mahogany floorboards, ebony furniture, and bedspreads in crisp cotton or raw silk complete the decor of discreet luxury.

The verandas, surrounded by exuberant vegetation, are furnished with rattan chairs, ideal in hot climates since they allow the air to circulate. At the end of the eighteenth century, the British colonists made furniture of only the finest and most expensive woods, including mahogany, rosewood, and violet wood. Some lovely craftsmanship can be seen in the carving of these sofas and chairs. Made for connoisseurs over a period of only about twenty years, these extremely rare chairs can now be found only in antique shops and auctions.

On the islands of the Indian Ocean, many of these colonial homes have been dismantled and moved several times during their life. Due to their wooden framework, these remarkable buildings could be dismantled piece by piece and rebuilt elsewhere. During the cholera and malaria epidemics of the nineteenth century, the residential buildings of Mauritius were moved to the country, like pawns on a chessboard, so that families could avoid the plague. The structures' mobility unfortunately brought on their disappearance, though there are still very fine examples in Mauritius, Seychelles, Réunion, and wherever else the dreams of the colonial empire builders led them.

PREVIOUS SPREAD, ABOVE, AND OPPOSITE:

NAMIBIA

Wolwedans, "the place where wolves dance," lies in a 4,500-square-mile reserve, split into two camps: Wolwedans Dune, composed of six tents, and Wolwedans Private Camp, a newlywed suite. The two areas enjoy a breathtaking view and exclusive comfort, though Wolwedans Private Camp, the more luxurious, has the advantage of allowing young couples complete privacy. The tents are built on wooden platforms and open onto the desert countryside, whose colors change as the day advances. The south of Namibia is particularly known for its dazzling beauty.

LEFT:

BOTSWANA

Kings Pool Camp overlooks a man-made lake frequented by hippos. The spacious suites are equipped with a bed/sitting room, a small private bath, and a *sala,* an exterior lounge where you can while away the time listening to the extraordinary sounds of African wildlife.

OPPOSITE:

SUBA, INDONESIA

Among the rice paddies and palm trees of the western part of the island, Claude Graves and his wife have created Nihiwatu, a small luxury hotel with eight bungalows and two villas, nestled into the tropical vegetation.

PREVIOUS SPREAD:

BALI

The Villa Balquisse is the ideal place to enjoy the charms of Balinese hospitality. The rooms' Javanese furniture is traditionally crafted in teak and coconut palm.

ABOVE AND OPPOSITE:

RAJASTHAN, INDIA

The national park of Ranthambore includes the luxury campsite of the Hotel Aman-I-Khas, an oasis of serenity in the open air. Under spacious, sophisticated tents, furniture of dark wood and tawny leather, cotton screens, a fan, muted lighting, and mats on the floor make for supreme comfort.

LEFT:

BALI

The Villa Balquisse, a hotel valued for its warm decoration, mixes Balinese and Javanese influences in its traditional architecture.

OPPOSITE:

BALI

In the open-plan residence of Anneke van Wesberghe, white curtains define separate spaces. In this guest room, a camp bed made of wood sits in front of a four-poster bed swathed in sheer cotton.

PREVIOUS SPREAD AND ABOVE:

MOKA, MAURITIUS

The Creole Eureka Mansion is one of the prettiest residences surviving in good condition from the colonial era. In room after room, magnificent furniture in finely carved precious woods—mahogany, ebony, rosewood—attests to the island's rich past. The wraparound veranda protects the house from heat and rain. The European colonials, who knew how to stay cool, ate

their meals here or entertained visitors with gin and tonics or tea while gazing out over the park.

The Eureka Mansion boasts 109 doors and windows, and all of the rooms communicate with each other. A rocking chair's back and seat are woven in various widths of rattan cane.

ABOVE LEFT:

GALLE, SRI LANKA

In the eighteenth century, the British colonists in Ceylon fashioned their furniture from the most expensive and most precious wood in the world, ebony. Several lovely examples of the area's beautiful woodcarving can be seen in Jean Hassid's residence.

ABOVE RIGHT:

GALLE, SRI LANKA

It was to an old Dutch residence that Charles Hulse decided to retire to write. In the writer's bedroom, a four-poster bed from the nineteenth century, draped in mosquito netting, is made of ebony. The floor is mahogany.

LEFT:

MOKA, MARITIUS

The bathroom in the Eureka Mansion holds a number of accessories from the colonial era: enamel basin, bathtub, and washstand.

THAILAND

In Bangkok, the place where legendary American businessman Jim Thompson lived is composed of six traditional houses, built of teak according to ancient construction techniques. The important collection of Asian art housed here testifies to the profound attachment Thompson felt to Thailand, where he made a fortune reviving the handwoven silk industry at the end of World War II. The beds are adorned with vibrantly colored Thai silk, a textile perfectly suited to the tropical climate because of its breathability.

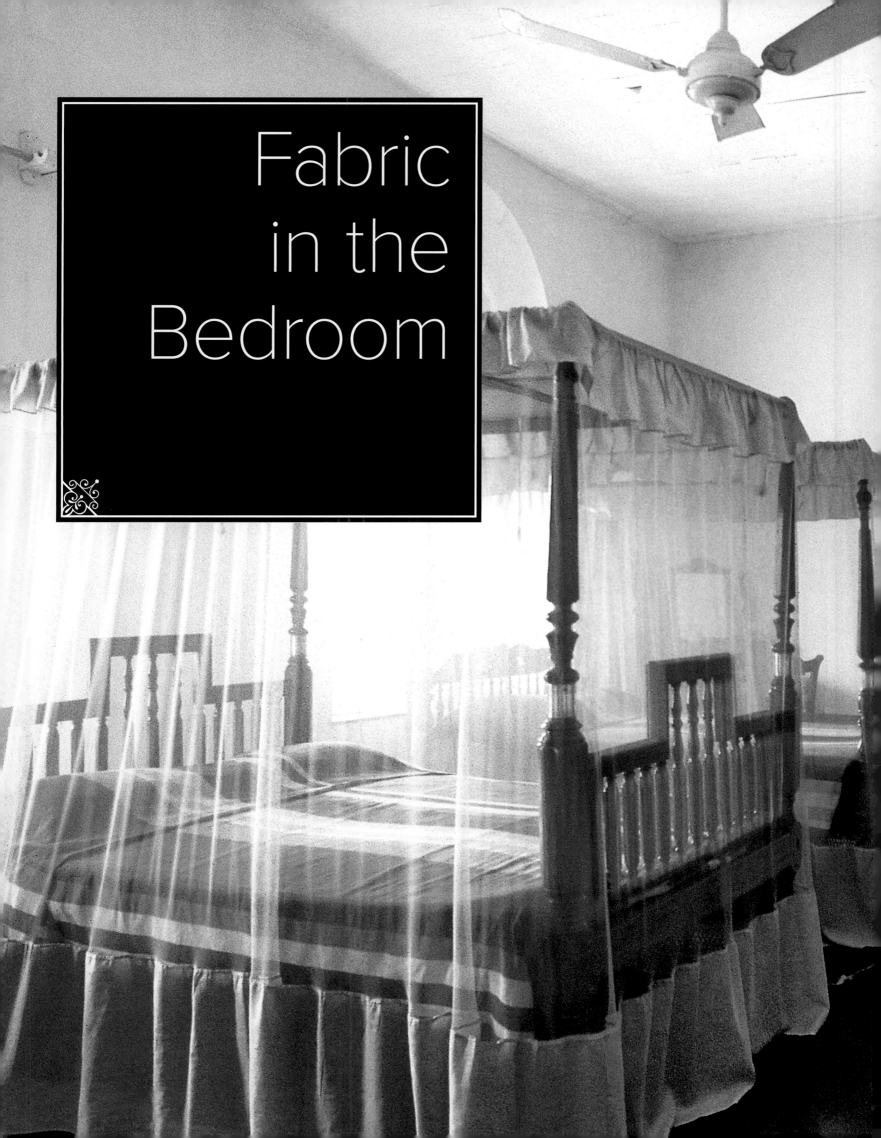

Fabric in the Bedroom

All over the planet, humankind has always found an outlet for artistic impulses in the creation of textiles. The most ancient civilizations learned to create textures, patterns, and above all colors in cloth, and showed a great sensitivity for fine fabrics. Throughout history, fabrics have played an important role in international trade, as they still do today. Used to represent a social position, a gift, or a geographic origin, or play a part in ceremonies attached to various stages of life, fabrics also occupy a privileged place in interior decoration, perhaps most of all in lounges and bedrooms. Whether monochrome or multicolored, cotton, silk, brocade, or muslin, the textiles in bedrooms reflect the basic human need for comfort and warmth in sleep.

It seems natural that the first monumental beds, as well as the first rooms specifically created for repose, should have been created in the countries with the coldest climates. In fact, the Nordic societies early on achieved an exceptional degree of comfort in their sleeping spaces. "Every bedroom had its bed which was covered with a comforter"—an accessory that is now de rigueur for beds in the West—explains Pascal Dibie in his book *Ethnologie de la chambre à coucher* (Ethnology of the Bedroom). He adds that the term *eiderdown* comes from the Icelandic *aedardun*.

Be that as it may, it is certain that all over the world, waking up in the morning in a bedroom bathed in natural light and softened with fabrics is the best way to start the day. Whether it's swathed in the lightest, sheerest voile, merely to preserve a little privacy, or in thicker, warmer, more tactile fabric when the days are short and chilly, the epicenter of the bedroom remains the bed. The bed should also be as comfortable as possible, neither too soft or too hard; after all, we spend a third of our lives sleeping. For a room of grand dimensions, we might choose a four-poster or domed, canopied *lit à la polonaise,* or a bed with a substantial headboard. For snug nights, some drape their bed with a grand canopy in their favorite material, suspended from steel rods fastened to the wall, while others have reinterpreted the canopy in a contemporary spirit by swathing the bed in translucent veils. The bedroom by nature is a very tactile place, where a generous range of textures and materials helps make things soft, comfortable, and cozy. All of these solutions, as we will see on the following pages, make their own vivid visual impression.

PREVIOUS SPREAD:

SRI LANKA

Mosquito netting envelops sleepers in tranquility during the divine hours of siesta or at night, while protecting them from biting insects.

ABOVE AND OPPOSITE:

ZANZIBAR

In Sylvia and Torgeir Vaage's house, diaphanous mosquito netting, ceiling fans, and heavy wooden shutters evoke the sweetness of life in the days of the sultanate, which became a British protectorate in 1890.

LEFT:

SEYCHELLES

There are few enclosed spaces here; the rooms are open on all sides to make the most of the cool ocean breeze.

PREVIOUS SPREAD:

LAMU, KENYA

In Anita Spoerri's house, delicate veils define an intimate zone not just around the bed but extending out into a large part of the room.

TOP:

MALINDI, KENYA

This colonial house looking out on the Indian Ocean, owned by Italo-Kenyan artist Armando Tanzini, delightfully mixes the ethnic and the classical with antique furniture from India, China, and the Indonesian island of Lombok.

BOTTOM:

KENYA

In Lamu, Anita Spoerri's bedroom regains its spacious openness when the curtains have been drawn back. In Manda, ecru cotton curtains clothe this small window with its frame of palm matting.

MANDA, KENYA

At Bruno Brighetti's Blue Safari Club, the frame of the bed's canopy is suspended
from the rafters in a room constructred entirely from natural materials. On the floor,
colorful rugs warm the room and provide softness under bare feet.

LAMU, KENYA

This residence was restored by Katharina Schmezer and
Hermann Stucki, following Swahili building traditions. The mango
wood four-poster was crafted by a local artisan. On the walls,
the colored wash evokes the *tadelakt* (lime wash) of Morocco.
Mashrabiya windows (traditional Arabic windows screened with
carved wood latticework) preserve privacy; the locally inspired
secretary is inlaid in bone.

TOP:

CONNECTICUT

The antiquarian Michael Trapp collects Greek columns and capitals, whole or in fragments. One of these decorates his bedroom. His passion for Greek antiquity inspired him to coat this room with layer upon layer of paint, to imitate as nearly as possible the look of ancient Greek architecture. Carefully chosen fabrics add to the overall effect.

BOTTOM:

CAPE TOWN

In this interior, the desire of owners Grant and Andrée to create a room of great drama, and to astound their guests, is vividly apparent.

OPPOSITE:

MARRAKECH

In the medina of the Red City, Belgian architect Quentin Wilbaux has given new life to secular houses while rigorously conforming to local traditional architecture. The wall hangings and the carpets covering the benches, mixed with Moroccan furniture, restore this bedroom to its original majesty.

ABOVE AND LEFT:

MARRAKECH

In Franca and Carla Sozzani's *riad* (a Moroccan guesthouse), cultures mix in the bedrooms, where richly colored precious fabrics blend with a zebra skin and local furniture.

OVERLEAF:

STOCKSFIELD, ENGLAND

Michael Chippendale, a stencil specialist, has ornamented this Ottoman bedroom with brass and gold stencils from floor to ceiling, a profusion of velvet and silk textures, and walls in shades of red and green, set off by an undercoat of metallic paint.

PROVENCE

In Lillian Williams's eighteenth-century folly, the bedroom walls and the Louis XVI furniture have been covered by the decorator Christian Dufour with a Laura Ashley print, which is gathered in a spectacular pleated sunburst on the ceiling. A Louis XV card table provides contrast.

PARIS

Known for his hats, Philippe Model is a personality in the world of fashion who also exercises his talents as a decorator. He is famous for the color line he created for a paint company, an interest he let loose on the walls of this apartment.

ABOVE:

SAINT-RÉMY, FRANCE

Concerned with the smallest of details, American painter Catherine Warren is very attentive to the subtleties of color. In this Provençal house, a joyous harmony emanates from a melange of styles—the eighteenth and nineteenth centuries, the 1930s and '40s. She balances classicism and the Baroque, gravity and exuberance, the formal and the informal.

LEFT:

PROVENCE

Earth tones and Provençal light inspired Agnès Comar, who in her eighteenth-century house uses monochrome fabrics in a stylishly simple design. The linen curtains, trimmed with organdy, hang on substantial horizontal rods. In this summer bedroom, white cotton curtains, cool and light, soften the wall, creating a backdrop for the bed. Fluid and luminous, they give a touch of softness and romance to the room.

PARIS

Fabric can easily be used as a wall covering. It's just as easy to mix contemporary and classical bedclothes, in a lighthearted play of contrasts.

VARZY, FRANCE

Built between 1672 and 1684 by Armand-François de Menou, following the plans of the architect Barthélemy Le Blanc, the Château de Menou has been called "the Versailles of the Nevers." It is now the home of Jean-Luc Gauzère and the celebrated decorator Jacques Garcia, who favor the seventeenth and eighteenth centuries, as this bedroom attests.

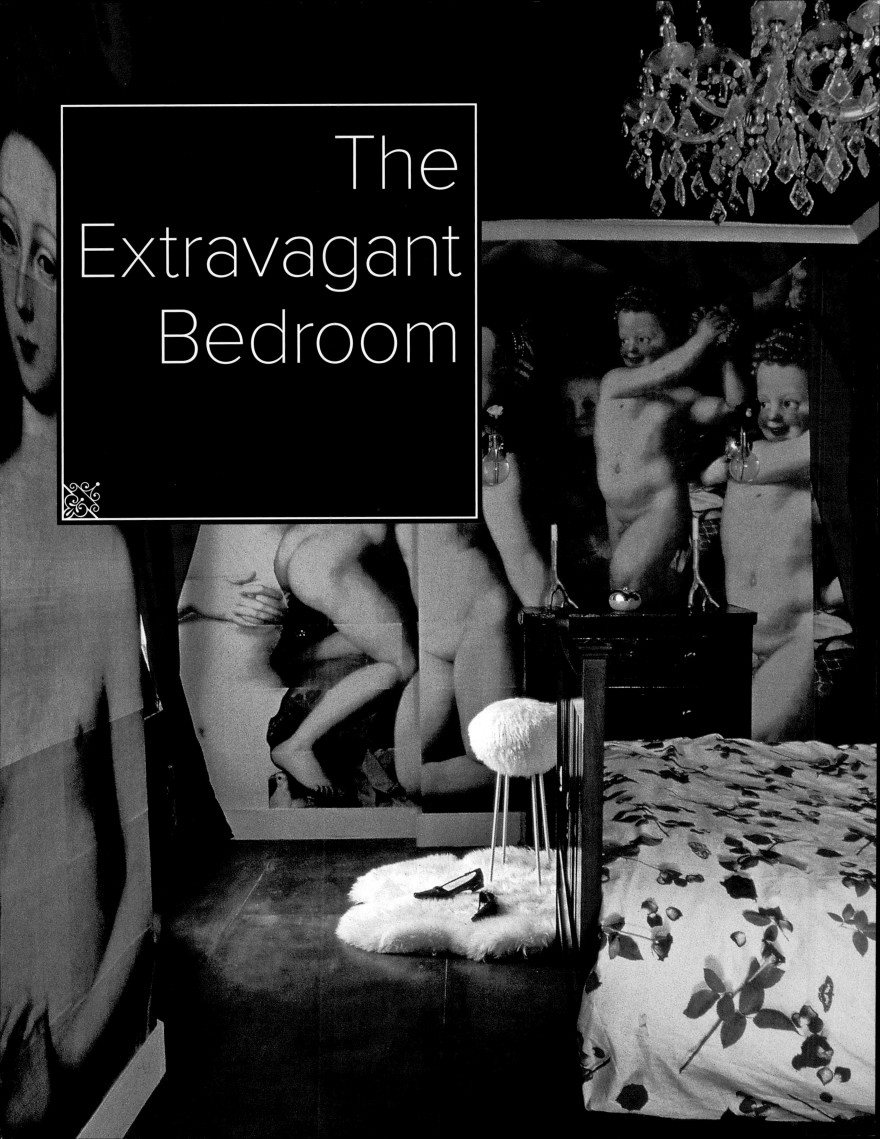

The Extravagant Bedroom

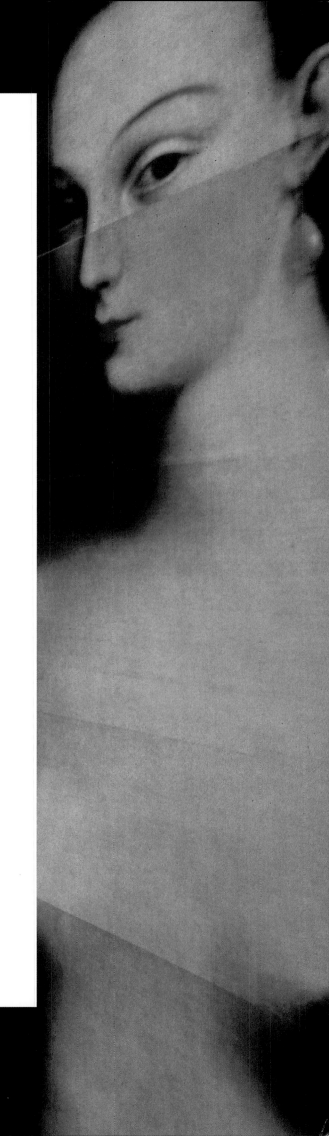

This chapter brings together a number of exceptional places. Originality, innovation, and above all free expression characterize these luxurious bedrooms, which revel in the language of the senses. Each offers a distinctive concept, using diverse materials, a wide range of colors, and a dizzying array of forms: from walls covered in reproductions to monumental Gothic architecture in trompe l'oeil, from a Manhattan apartment inspired by Byzantine art to a room devoted to the sumptuous spirit of the eighteenth century.

The owners, interior decorators, and artists represented here have given the best of themselves—not only their work, but also their cultural background and understanding of the world—through decor, design, and art. Here we are not merely viewing a gallery of bedrooms, as visitors trying to penetrate their intimacy; rather, we seek to come closer to these master designers, those who usually create for others, and perhaps try to unveil their mysteries. It is through their own houses that we can best understand the creators of dreams.

Many such creators from all corners of the globe have agreed to open the door to us, to let us see the private spaces that are often something of a laboratory, where they experiment with the concepts they may later use for their clients. Or perhaps it is the opposite—that is, here they can express ideas for themselves alone, which may never see light in a client's home. In short, here they reveal in their own homes their dream of the ideal bedroom, in which they have only one goal: to be happy. Raymond Isidore, known as Little Picasso, who for thirty years has patiently covered his small house in fragments of glass and china, is one of these creators. Niki de Saint-Phalle, with her Empress, a structure of concrete decorated with glass and mirror mosaic that housed both her house and studio, is another.

If we consider for a moment these interiors as documents of the history of taste, they might signify the triumph of the spectacular. What strikes the viewer first is their extravagance, and then their pleasure in exhibitionism, in narcissism, in the expression of the subconscious.

More than any other, these artists have been able to create eccentric spaces, set their own rules, perfect an ideal of the art of living—or at the very least create an illusion of it. From Cairo to Vienna by way of Moscow, London, and Aleppo, here are icons of design, creations of an aesthetic that is resolutely hybrid, with an eye to stagecraft and to the theatrical. The result: a succession of fascinating images and unexpected discoveries

PREVIOUS SPREAD:

LONDON

Carolyn Corben's bedroom expresses her dreamy and passionate temperament, with walls covered with enlarged reproductions of the paintings *Gabrielle d'Estrées and One of Her Sisters* and *An Allegory of Love*. Above, a crystal chandelier found in a flea market; on the floor, a little white sheepskin rug.

OPPOSITE, TOP:

PARIS

The space Luc and Géraldine Deschamps have dedicated to sleep is entirely wrapped in fabric. On the wall, an eighteenth-century painting.

OPPOSITE, BOTTOM:

CUERNAVACA, MEXICO

In Martha Yolanda Quezada's residence, designed by architect Alberto Kalach, a painting by Abel Quezada, her husband, dominates the bedroom wall.

RIGHT:

CAPE TOWN

Packed with contemporary African art, Michael and Anthea Methven's house bears witness to their fascination with life-size animal sculptures. Above the headboard, constructed of a line of wooden statues, is a Michael Methven lamp of paper stretched over a wire frame.

PREVIOUS SPREAD:

LONDON

More than a bold association of styles, epochs, and colors, the work of Hassan Abdullah, a former interior designer who is now a restaurateur, is an inventive staging of furniture. Highlights include a gilded wooden headboard and a French dressing table from the 1920s.

LEFT AND ABOVE:

PARIS

The Spanish origins of the designer Serge Olivares are apparent in his red and black bedroom. Previously a textile designer, he presently renovates antique furniture, like this Louis XVI chair with the original finish, reupholstered in silk and ornamented with a fan of plumes on the seat and opera embroidery on its back.

RIGHT AND ABOVE:

VIENNA

Steffan Riedl's apartment, decorated with great freedom, is laid out like a fabulous history of European decorative arts. On the walls of this guest room is a monumental Gothic architectural trompe l'oeil executed by the owner himself.

ABOVE:

TUSCANY

Celebrated contemporary artist Niki de Saint-Phalle first became known for her *Nanas,* archetypal mother figures, often sculpted of papier mâché. At the end of the 1970s, she traveled to Tuscany to create the large Tarot Garden sculpture park along with other artists. From the giant womb of the Empress, a sphinx-shaped concrete structure covered in glass and mirror mosaic that housed her house and studio, the artist could admire the landscape.

LEFT:

CAIRO

The twenty-eight windows of Hugh Sowden's pavilion were found on a visit to the attic of a Turkish palace in Mazrouna. The Belle Époque–style four-poster is draped with damask silk.

LEFT AND ABOVE:

FRANCE, NEAR CHARTRES

Raymond Isidore, known as "Little Picasso," was a custodian at a cemetery, a job he did not much care for. When his workday was over, he dedicated himself to decorating his small house, completely covered with a mosaic of ceramic and glass fragments.

OPPOSITE:

BOMBAY

In this bedroom of the couturiers and interior designers Abu Jani and Sandeep Khosla, the sculpted bed is an antique from southern India. On the wall to the right is an imposing painting of the lotus of Ramachandra, covering four panels. Despite the abundance of precious objects, works of art, and rich materials (bronze, silver, and gold), the room has an air of serenity. The substantial carved silver doors are from Gujarat.

OPPOSITE AND ABOVE:

MOSCOW

The dreamy wallpaper, embroidered bedspread, and lamps (their own creation) are the only decorations that Paul Mathieu and Michael Ray brought to this apartment. They found the icons, suitcases, and Russian easels, which now find use as bedside tables, already in place here.

OVERLEAF:

BRUSSELS

Christophe Decarpentr e's bedroom is strongly influenced by the Spanish Baroque. The Venetian portico is crnamented with a mirror, the marble busts date from the seventeenth century, and the ivory tower is French, from 1830.

NORMANDY

The artist Ramuntcho de Saint-Amand spends most of his time in a small presbytery built in 1840, near Dieppe. He loves the idea of the sumptuous bedroom of the eighteenth century, and the boudoirs where one had tea and conversation, so much that he has installed a bed in each of six rooms. An impressive number of statues occupy the rooms: busts, heads, men, women, medallions.

ABOVE AND RIGHT:

In the attic, a nineteenth-century bed under exposed beams is covered in fabric ornamented with cameos created for Pierre Frey.

OPPOSITE:

Ramuntcho de Saint-Amand's plaster statues, most of them more than a hundred years old, were collected over a period of twenty years. The spirit of the eighteenth century still dominates this bedroom.

PREVIOUS SPREAD:

LONDON

In 1979 Dennis Seevers acquired a London house dating to 1724, which he decorated meticulously to re-create the daily life of an eighteenth-century silk manufacturer. Scattered objects, an unmade bed, and lit candles give the feeling that the owner has only just left the room. This staging is open to the public.

OPPOSITE AND RIGHT:

ALEPPO, SYRIA

Julien Jalal Eddine Weiss, a Frenchman, has become a virtuoso of the table zither, or *quanun,* after having studied with masters from Egypt, Tunisia, Turkey, Lebanon, Syria, and Iraq. In the heart of Aleppo, he has made a home in a fourteenth-century Mameluke palace, where he hosts a regular salon for traditional music, when he is not traveling through Europe with other Oriental musicians. In his bedrooms, Syrian furniture, inlaid with mother-of-pearl, coexists harmoniously with shimmering fabrics and rugs.

OPPOSITE:

NEW YORK

The masculine note of a Herter Brothers bed carries on a subtle dialogue with a Miró painting. According to owner Joseph Holtzman, the former editor of *Nest*, a design magazine, white walls are too boring. He prefers them painted, and completely covered—not to say cluttered—to the last square inch.

RIGHT:

PARIS

A crown is suspended above Marie Beltrami's bed to theatrical effect. The bedside tables are antiqued in puce. The stippled walls have been washed with water mixed with gold paint.

OVERLEAF:

LE NEUBOURG, FRANCE

Jacques Garcia has arranged this room in the Château Champ de Bataille in the sumptuous spirit of the seventeenth century. His bed, a seventeenth-century *lit à la duchesse,* with tester and curtains only at the head, is covered in fabric of the same period, embroidered with Chinese motifs on silk. Above the miniature *couleuvrine* (cannon) from the army of the count of Toulouse on the mantel is an inlaid and bronzed Boulle wall clock.

PREVIOUS SPREAD:

LONDON

Virginia Bates owns a vintage clothing boutique in Holland Park, and the house she lives in is something of an extension of her store. Her bedroom, where exotic textiles abound, is what she might have dreamed of as a small child—enchanting, opulent, with a touch of madness.

LEFT AND ABOVE:

NEW YORK

In her Manhattan apartment, Mary McFadden was inspired by early Byzantine architecture, such as the fourth-century chapel built for the Emperor Constantine in his palace. With the help of artist Joseph Stashkevetch, she has ornamented her bedroom with an ancient circular calendar on the gilded ceiling; she designed the totemic black chairs herself. The stencils used for the painted wall design were created by Stashkevetch specifically for McFadden.

OPPOSITE:

LUXOR, EGYPT

With architect Olivier Sednaoui, Zeina Abou Kheir directed the construction of the Hotel Al Moudira with 150 artisans and workers. The Ottoman bed is of royal dimensions. The walls are painted with natural pigments in a palette of ocher and red, along with the precise shade of blue used in the houses and temples of ancient Egypt. The frescoes are the creation of Mario Dahabi.

The Minimalist Bedroom

Pared down to the essentials, the minimalist bedroom is often decorated in contemporary style, sometimes with custom-made furniture or original designer pieces. Natural materials such as wood, stone, or tiles are set against the clean, restrained backdrop of white walls. Long white cotton voile curtains swathe the bed and windows, filtering the light at the end of the day for a cool, serene atmosphere.

Here and on the pages that follow, you will find contrasting examples of extreme sophistication, from the sleek style of the contemporary bedroom shown on this spread to the absolute austerity of a room decorated according to ancestral tradition. In the first, a large black headboard dominates an entire section of wall, and a designer fireplace is highlighted with geometric reliefs. Toward the end of the chapter, we visit an Egyptian oasis where both architecture and decoration use the same elemental materials—sandstone, crystallized salt, palm wood, and earth—that have been used for two thousand years. Behind heavy doors, neutral tones contrast with the deeper notes of wood. With no telephone, no electricity even, this is a space utterly outside time. Despite the distance between these worlds, though, in both places we find ourselves in a universe at once monumental and personal, a dream bedroom.

Then there is the minimalist Indian chic of an eighteenth-century palace near Udaipur, or a contemporary Indian residence irresistible to the eye. The Mongol arches, the finely wrought niches, and the stone sculptures all defer to the asceticism of the room.

Across the restraint common to these different places, we can draw the major axes of the refined bedroom. Wood, a material that is universal and timeless, claims an ever-increasing presence in these rooms. Its potent decorative power makes it the best material to create an ascetic look that is still not overly austere. A bedroom entirely paneled in wood, with the bed incorporated into a podium, is a good example. Notice the extreme economy of furniture. Farther on, a monastic bedroom grabs our attention, in an airy architectural setting of great purity.

Finally, in Japan, where the principles of Zen Buddhism strip away everything that is not essential, we admire the rice paper screens, the diaphanous lighting, the tatami mats. Somehow, strangely, these intensely traditional materials do not give the impression of being in any way things of the past. On the contrary, it is difficult to imagine an environment more modern. We have the sensation of seeing traditional Japan resurfacing in this magnificent bedroom through its grand simplicity and its Zen refinement. A visual enlightenment . . .

PREVIOUS SPREAD:

NEWCASTLE-UPON-TYRE, ENGLAND

In Carolyn and Christian van Outersterp's bedroom, the accent is on the sculptural fireplace and the bed's black moleskin headboard.

ABOVE AND LEFT:

ASILAH, MOROCCO

In this immaculate Dubois family bedroom, a deep divan is decorated with cushions of different sizes. A *futa* (cloth worn as a wraparound skirt) embroidered with red borders acts as a curtain. On the shelf are Ibo sculptures from Nigeria. The window openings are the size of small dormer windows.

OPPOSITE, TOP:

CAPE TOWN

This contemporary residence was designed by the architect Greg Wright for a couple who see minimalism as a way of life, devoid of ornamentation and superfluous details.

OPPOSITE, BOTTOM:

LONDON

In architect Voon Wong's apartment, the TV unit is integrated into the wall to minimize its impact.

ABOVE AND OPPOSITE:

MIDI, FRANCE

According to architect Claudio Silvestrin, the beauty of a room depends more on the essence of its structure than on colors, fabrics, and furniture. For Armand Bartos, he has created a monastic bedroom, more serene than austere.

OVERLEAF:

PARIS

A bed entirely covered in leopard skins is the only furnishing in this bedroom.

PREVIOUS SPREAD:

LOS ANGELES

Harriet Selling's simple futon lies on a massive wooden platform, fitted with deep drawers in the front.

LEFT AND ABOVE:

SHIKOKU, JAPAN

In sculptor-designer Isamu Noguchi's renovated seventeenth-century samurai house, the bedroom is a sweeping space for practicing daily meditation. Movable screens make the space fluid and flexible. Noguchi's Akari hanging paper lamps suffuse the room with soft light.

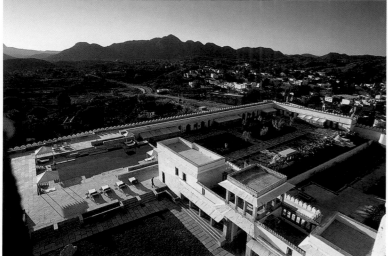

UDAIPUR, INDIA

In ancient Rajasthan, some princely residences, like the fortified palace of Devi Gar, have been transformed into hotels. Purchased a few years ago by the Poddar family, the palace has been renovated by the architects Gautam Bhatia and Navin Gupta. Perched on the Aravali hills, its generous interior spaces, perfect for relaxation, are decorated in luxurious Indian minimalism.

LAMU, KENYA

A restrained elegance characterizes this interior
with its ocher walls and floors, created by designers
Hermann Stucki and Katharina Schmezer.

SIWA, EGYPT

Five hundred miles west of Cairo, Siwa is the most intriguing and attractive oasis in the Sahara. In this idyllic setting, situated between spectacular sandstone mountains and the edge of a lake, the humanist environmentalist Mounir Neamatalla decided to create Hotel Adrère Amellal in the form of a traditional village. Building without a plan, with the help of local artisans, he used only materials available in the area—sandstone, earth, salt crystal, palm wood. To complete his dream, he called on the talented interior designer India Mahdavi. The beds and bedside tables of woven palm as well as the large striped floor rugs were also locally produced.

LEFT AND ABOVE:

NEW DELHI

In Lekha and Ranjan Poddar's bedroom, the walls are made of masonry brick set in bands, and the floor is of varnished Burmese teak. A row of narrow, shuttered vertical openings allows natural light to filter through. Above the bed, also made of teak, is a modern painting by V. S. Gaitonde. For the design of this house—a complex structure of concrete, brick, iron, copper, and glass—the owners chose two daring young architects, Inni Chatterjee and Samiir Wheaton. The elephant in the foreground is a creation of the Indian artist Bharti Kher.

OVERLEAF:

SICILY

At the Hotel Atelier sul Mare, the Prophet bedroom, designed by Antonio Presti, the owner, with Bario Bellezza and Adele Cambria, is dedicated to film director and writer Pier Paolo Pasolini. The red clay walls are decorated with Arabic calligraphy.

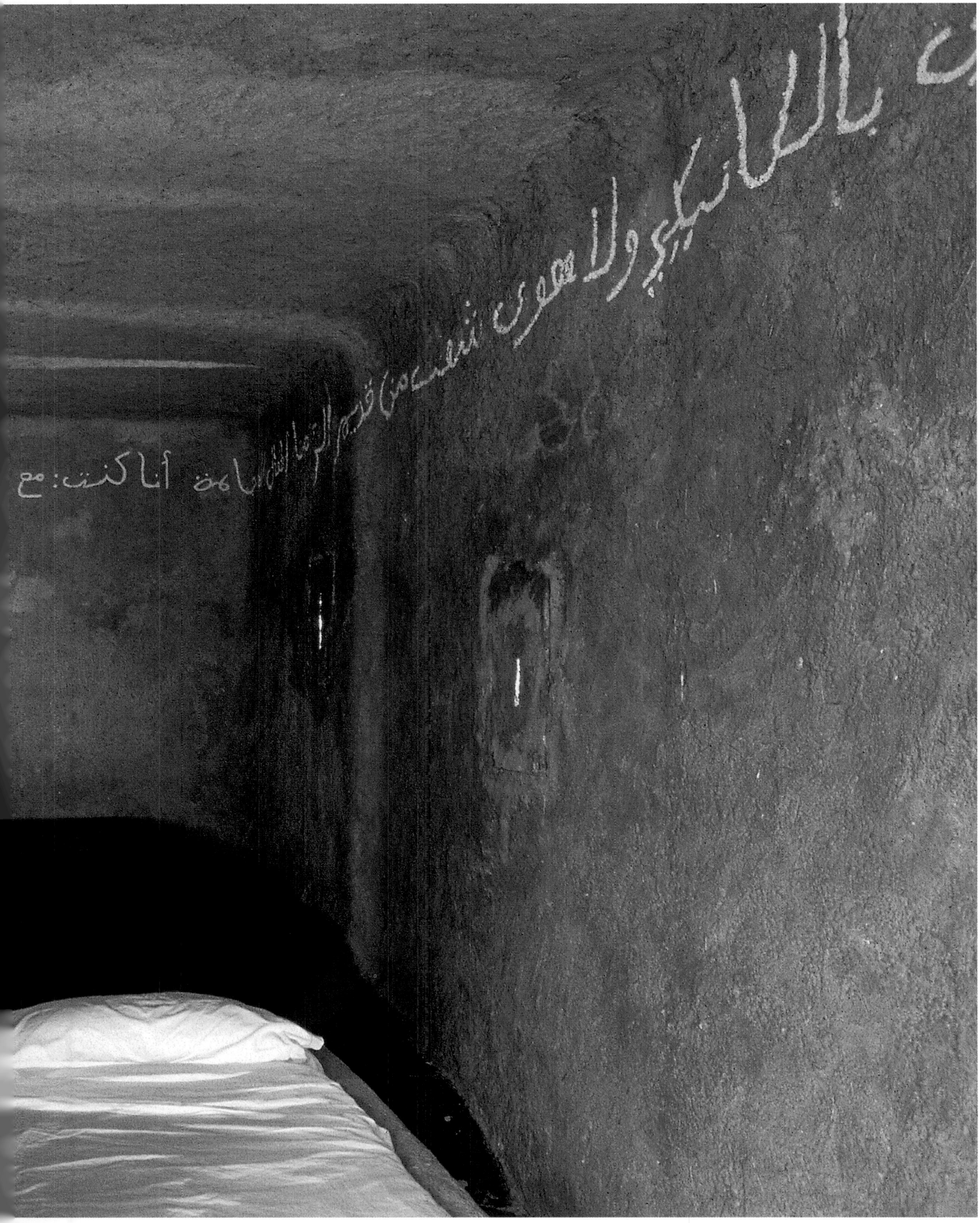
أنا كنت: مع

The
Enclosed
Bed

Sheltered, secure in our own space, we are no longer out in the open, no longer exposed; we have no more need to put up a front. We can shut ourselves away, put on clothing that is old, comfortable, or ridiculous—or wear nothing at all if the weather is warm. We might be isolated, both socially and physically, but this isolation nevertheless brings a certain comfort. In the intimacy of our bedrooms, we are sheltered from cold, from drafts, from the heat and harsh light—and beds curtained with fabric, or set into alcoves, are the ultimate expression of the desire for such shelter.

If we take a trip back into the past, to the houses of Pompeii, we find the first alcove bedrooms. The master of the household had at his disposal a number of sleeping chambers, arranged around an interior courtyard, the direction they faced determining whether they were used as summer or winter chambers. However, as ethnologist Pascal Dibie explains, "the placement of the bed was usually indicated by a raised area in the floor and a vault above, unless the alcove was marked on the floor with white blocks of marble or other stone."

After the austerity of the Middle Ages, bedroom aesthetics took a step forward around the end of the fifteenth century, when the large communal beds of the bourgeois yielded to private beds. The bed itself took on more prestige at the same time, often becoming the most substantial financial investment in the home. With their carved wood and turned columns, some Renaissance beds are veritable works of art, monuments of the interior that measure up to ten feet across. Their vast size was amply accentuated by a number of cushions, and above all by elegant sliding bed curtains. These canopy beds or four-posters flaunt an unprecedented sense of ease and luxury.

But it was during the reign of Louis XIV that the bed reached its height of sophistication, with the ceremonial bed. It was no longer a matter merely of sculpted wooden beds, but of "swags of velvet trimmed with gold and plumes of feathers atop the bedposts." The curtains, creating a border between the private and public space, could be pulled back to transform the bedroom into a reception room. This style survived until the first quarter of the eighteenth century, when it was dropped in favor of the more open *lit à la duchesse,* with tester and curtains only at the head, and other, simpler canopied beds. It was in the middle of the eighteenth century, too, that the bedroom became a place used only for sleeping, the room we know today.

Today, the enclosed bed continues to evolve as contemporary styles emerge, ranging from clean-lined boxy forms covered in fabric to modern nests tucked into alcoves. The following pages invite you to discover these, and many more.

PREVIOUS SPREAD:

TEL AVIV

A clean-lined, boxy contemporary bed curtained in panels of sheer fabric, by Andrée Putman.

ABOVE:

PARIS

An alcove entirely sheathed in white tile, designed by the contemporary artist Jean-Pierre Raynaud.

LEFT:

PARIS

The distinctive style of Gaetano Pesce has left its mark on everything in an apartment that belonged to Marc André Hubin. The master bed is mounted on casters and entirely encased in a down-filled cover. The luminous glass balls were created by the master glassblowers of Murano.

SICILY

The Egg bedroom at the Hotel Atelier sul Mare is a masterpiece in itself. Designed by the sculptor Paolo Icaro, the bed creates a nest, filling the entire space. A simple change of place no longer suffices for the adventurous traveler; the decor itself must provide transport to another world.

TOP:

PARIS

Sliding panels of fabric on metal rods separate a bedroom area styled by Andrée Putman, filtering and softening the light that floods the apartment through the large windows.

BOTTOM:

JOHANNESBURG

The austere beauty of Dead Vlei, a dry lake in Namibia where the sculptural trunks of ancient acacias punctuate the cracked lake bed, inspired the designer Laurie Owen. Her bedroom is suffused with the aged ivory and chalk white hues of this arid land.

ESSAOUIRA, MOROCCO

In Joël Martial's bedroom, the bed rests on a masonry base. The walls are subtly tinted a warm pale cream. Toile curtains separate the space reserved for sleeping from the rest of the room.

PREVIOUS SPREAD:

PONDICHERRY, INDIA

In Françoise Gérin's house, a double four-poster bed swathed in mosquito netting creates an intimate space.

ABOVE AND RIGHT:

MARRAKECH

In this bedroom in Dar Kawa that opens directly onto an interior courtyard, the distressed metal bed is set into an alcove delineated by a stucco arch. The hand-sewn bedspread was made by Valérie Barkowski. On the floor is a straw and wool rug made in Khemisset, near Meknes.

SOUTH OF NEW DELHI

The *jharokas,* or projecting balconies, punctuated by columns, of two *havelis* glimpsed in the distance first stirred interest in the Indian artist Aman Nath and his friend, businessman Francis Wacziarg. Fifteen years later these two seventeenth- and eighteenth-century residences have regained their splendor. A gallery opening onto a courtyard has become an integral part of this bedroom. A hammock is suspended from the ceiling, while the bed is tucked into an alcove. Ancient wooden doors and statues complete the decor.

ABOVE AND LEFT:

LUXOR, EGYPT

The residence of Christian Louboutin, designed by Olivier Sednaoui, melds perfectly with the Egyptian countryside. Like the surrounding mountains, it turns from an oatmeal shade in the morning to a blinding white in the hottest hours of the day, to become tinged with rose in the evening. Its architecture of mud-walled vaults and domes is a vibrant homage to the celebrated Egyptian architect Hassan Fathy. In the earth-toned bedroom, the bed glows with color under a dome with arched openings.

OPPOSITE:

LUXOR, EGYPT

A king-size Ottoman-style bed in the Hotel Al Moudira is accented with a precious Central Asian *suzani,* a hand-embroidered silk hanging, which carries on a subtle dialogue with the splendid frescoes by artist Mario Dahabi. Architect Olivier Sednaoui made use of traditional Arabic architecture, with its sweeping curves and arched, domed ceilings.

PREVIOUS SPREAD:

LAMU, KENYA

In the eighteenth-century Swahili house restored and decorated by Hermann Stucki and Katharina Schmezer, palm leaves are woven over the wooden frame of a camp bed. The bed linens and the curtains hanging from a heavy eighteenth-century wooden rod were created by African silk manufacturers. The floor is entirely covered in prayer mats traditionally used in mosques.

LEFT:

LAMU, KENYA

In the bedroom of owners Hermann Stucki and Katharina Schmezer, the ancient bed, a local find, is entirely enclosed in luminous sheer silk mosquito netting; the bedspread is an Indian sari. On the floor is a splendid *mkeka,* a rare rug hand-woven in Tanzania.

OPPOSITE, TOP:

BALI

In this bedroom in a converted attic space, decoration is kept to a bare minimum so as not to detract from the wooden Balinese bed.

OPPOSITE, BOTTOM:

TUNIS

In Tunisia, the woodwork that frames this bed is called a "hairdresser's salon" because of its resemblance to the display windows once common at hairdressers and barbershops. This one belongs to Jean-Pierre and Zeineb Marcie-Rivière.

BALI

The omnipresence of wood lends a charming simplicity to the Balinese bedroom of Annelies and Jean-Jacques Audureau, given a touch of warmth by the soft hues of silk cushions.

DEOGARH, INDIA

Deogarh Mahal, an ancient fortified palace, has been transformed into a hotel by the present owner, Rawar Nahar Singh. In this jewel-toned bedroom, a raised mattress set into an alcove projecting from the palace's facade invites repose.

OPPOSITE:

DEOGARH, INDIA

The nineteenth-century Indian palace of Deogarh Mahal has been renovated with great attention to authenticity. This bedroom has regained its former opulence with a richly decorated tile ceiling and delicately carved woodwork.

ABOVE:

BOMBAY

This boudoir is one of the guest rooms in the residence of fashion designers Abu Jani and Sandeep Khosla, who wanted to create a sensuous and intoxicating atmosphere. The centerpiece of this place is a monumental antique Portuguese *lit clos*, or box bed, made of carved sandalwood in the north of India. It is covered in a bedspread and cushions made of fur. A silver platter and a Bohemian crystal goblet complete the picture.

LEFT AND ABOVE:

NEUBOURG, FRANCE

At the Château Champ de Bataille, the romance of the Age of Reason and the taste for comfort of the English manor house come together in the work of the talented decorator Jacques Garcia. Here, wooden Louis XV *lits clos* (enclosed beds) are draped with early-nineteenth-century fabric; the rugs are designed by Jacques Garcia.

OVERLEAF:

MIDI, FRANCE

The painter Hervé Thibault has succeeded in suffusing his home with a soft atmosphere full of poetry. To accentuate the bedroom's intimate quality, the bed, over which is suspended a baldachin in tones of gold and bluish gray echoed in the bedcoverings, is set into a recess in the room, an alcove. The woodwork and the double doors pick up the gold and gray tones of the bed. An impressive collection of Chinese terra-cotta jars is arrayed on the chest of drawers.

The Classical Bedroom

Isn't the bedroom the perfect place to relax, to nap, to sleep, to make love? Still, when we slip between the sheets, we are only doing what has been done since the beginning of humankind. A short journey back through the highlights of the history of sleeping spaces will help us better understand the origins and evolution of the bed.

The history of the bed—not only the development of its physical form, but also its central role in society—is absolutely fascinating. If ancient Rome embodied the civilization of the bed, with beds for sleeping, reading, writing, eating, and entertaining, the ideal in the Middle Ages was a bed that could be dismantled and taken along on its owner's travels. The medieval bed was wide and short; this was because people slept sitting up at that time, lying down being reserved for sickness and death. Such a bed, hung with curtains that could be drawn back during the day and closed again at night, was often the most valuable piece of furniture in a household. The concept of a box (the bed) inside another box (the bedroom) persisted for a long time. And not only was one supposed to welcome guests into the medieval bed, offering them the warmth and protection of this enclosed space, but on feudal land, peasants were obliged to offer such hospitality to their overlords.

Centuries later, Louis XIV established what would come to be known as the ceremonial bed, creating a sharper separation between private and public space, as well as between man and woman. This bed was to become a sacred object, and at the same time the linchpin for a strong social order. In the grand bedroom of the king, a balustrade divided the room in two, demarcating the line between the intimate and the public—a symbolic border, yet viscerally understood.

The king's bed was large—immense, in fact—and set "on end"; that is, the long side was set against the wall. It was also lavishly hung with heavy drapes that protected its sleeping occupant from drafts and chilly air. The same kind of bed could be found in the queen's room, indicating a system of two separate bedrooms. But this separation of the sexes was no longer the standard under Louis Philippe (1773-1850), a monarch who initiated a revolution in the bedroom. The "Citizen King," an inveterate traveler, returned from one of his trips to England determined to establish the British custom of the shared bedroom and the matrimonial bed in France, applying this concept at both the Louvre and the Chateau d'Eu, where he set up a marital bedroom with a very large bed.

Two elements of this revolution in bed form would endure all the way up to the twenty-first century: the bed's increased comfort, and its height. Great attention was given to thick mattresses, stuffed according to the seasons with horsehair, wool, cotton, and even silk. The bed was so high that it had to be furnished with stepstools. Today no one climbs up to a bed; in fact, more often we fall into bed instead. But in some places, traces of that epoch still endure: the "king-size bed," popular in luxury hotel rooms, and decorative bedcurtains, which evoke the whimsically arched and canopied *lit à la polonaise,* or "Polish bed."

One of the eighteenth-century bedrooms in the Château de Morson, which Ted and Lillian Williams fell in love with at first sight.

LEFT AND ABOVE:

NORMANDY, FRANCE

The Château de Morson, built in 1750 by the marquis de Morson, is one of the rare follies still intact in France, as many were sacked during the French Revolution. Its restoration nevertheless took ten years. On the lavishly canopied eighteenth-century bed, the wooden frame is painted white to match the decorative wall trim. A small card table on long curved legs makes an elegant accent.

OPPOSITE AND RIGHT:

MIDI, FRANCE

The ancient hunting lodge of the archbishop of Avignon, a Provençal folly surrounded by magnificent gardens, was restored by Lillian and Ted Williams, Americans who are passionate about eighteenth-century decorative arts and fabrics. The *lit à la polonaise,* or "Polish bed," a style in vogue during the Age of Reason, is domed and canopied in golden yellow fabric. During this period, floral designs were also very popular.

OVERLEAF:

GERS, FRANCE

In this eighteenth-century bedroom at the Château de Bonas, with its lovely parquet floor, the Restoration-era bed fits snugly in an alcove. On the mantel, an eighteenth-century Sèvres bisque clock and some porcelain from the same era.

CHÂTEAU DE THOIRY, FRANCE

In the sixteenth century, Raoul Moreau built this château to create a favorable environment for his alchemical studies. Through its careful positioning on the site and its architectural proportions, as well as the play of mirrors, of light and shade, the château was designed to blend in with—even to become one with—the universe. Sunlight seems to inhabit the house, streaming in through the windows to the heart of the interior. This voluptuous and refined bedroom invites us to immerse ourselves in the art of living in the Age of Reason.

149

OPPOSITE:

GERS, FRANCE

This hushed bedroom, in colors conducive
to resting and relaxing, fits naturally into the
eighteenth-century setting of the Château
de Bonas, designated a historic monument.

ABOVE:

PARIS

A man of the theater, Alexandre Vassiliev
has designed his apartment like a stage
set. Entering this space is like stepping into
imperial Russia. The Louis Philippe sleigh bed
in mahogany veneer is draped with striped
cotton and covered with nineteenth-century
cashmere spreads. Engraved portraits of
Russian generals, an 1840s opaline chandelier, and a Danish Empire mirror are among
the many sumptuous items that fill the room.

OPPOSITE AND LEFT:

PROVENCE

In the Alpilles, the decorator Liza Kessel has given new life to a splendid Napoleon III canopy bed, found in an antiques store in the United States by the owner of the house. The bed's original cloth canopy has been removed to better reveal the refined details of the ironwork frame. For the floor, wide planks of rough fir were painstakingly stained to create a very subtle grayish white finish. The large rug that partially covers the floor was bought at a souk in Istanbul. An eclectic collection of frames and mirrors in various sizes and shapes adds to the personality of this room.

In another bedroom of the same house, a rich selection of fabrics gives great character to the space.

OPPOSITE AND BOTTOM LEFT:

BETZ, FRANCE

At the Château Collinances, a sunny bedroom in white and gold has been created in a seventeenth-century caretaker's apartment. The walls are delicately decorated in the German Renaissance style by artist Pierre Peyrolle. A pair of Medici vases gilded in gold leaf takes pride of place on either side of the fireplace.

ABOVE AND BOTTOM RIGHT:

PARIS

For the company Chez Vous, a business based in Sausalito, California, Myra Hoefer has decorated dozens of Parisian apartments for rent, all situated in Saint-Germain-des-Prés, the most desirable area for foreign guests. In this one, she has brought together a number of French antiques, a voluptuous contemporary bed, and cream silk taffeta curtains. The shades of white and beige make for a soft, comforting atmosphere.

PREVIOIUS SPREAD:

LUBERON, FRANCE

In this bedroom, two French bisque bathing girls from 1900 pose on a Gustavian table. The bed and the chairs are also rustic Gustavian; the stools, from the same era, are quite rare. The painting, titled *Crovaca di Roma,* is by Arne Tengblad, co-owner of the place with Anna Bonde.

LEFT:

GERS, FRANCE

Katharina Schmezer and Hermann Stucki have combined their talents to decorate this room, covering the bed with rich, subtly striped fabrics.

OPPOSITE:

PARIS

A former collaborator of Karl Lagerfeld, fashion designer Vincent Darré loves hunting for extraordinary objects in antiques shops. His Parisian apartment is a paean to a sublimely sophisticated civilization, an elegant Europe all but lost today, summed up in a few fragments of vintage silk, some Aubusson tapestries, and sculpted wood.

OVERLEAF:

BONNIEUX, FRANCE

In this house in the Luberon mountains, Wiveka Piper has created a soft atmosphere around a pair of Gustavian beds, painted a subtle pale taupe.

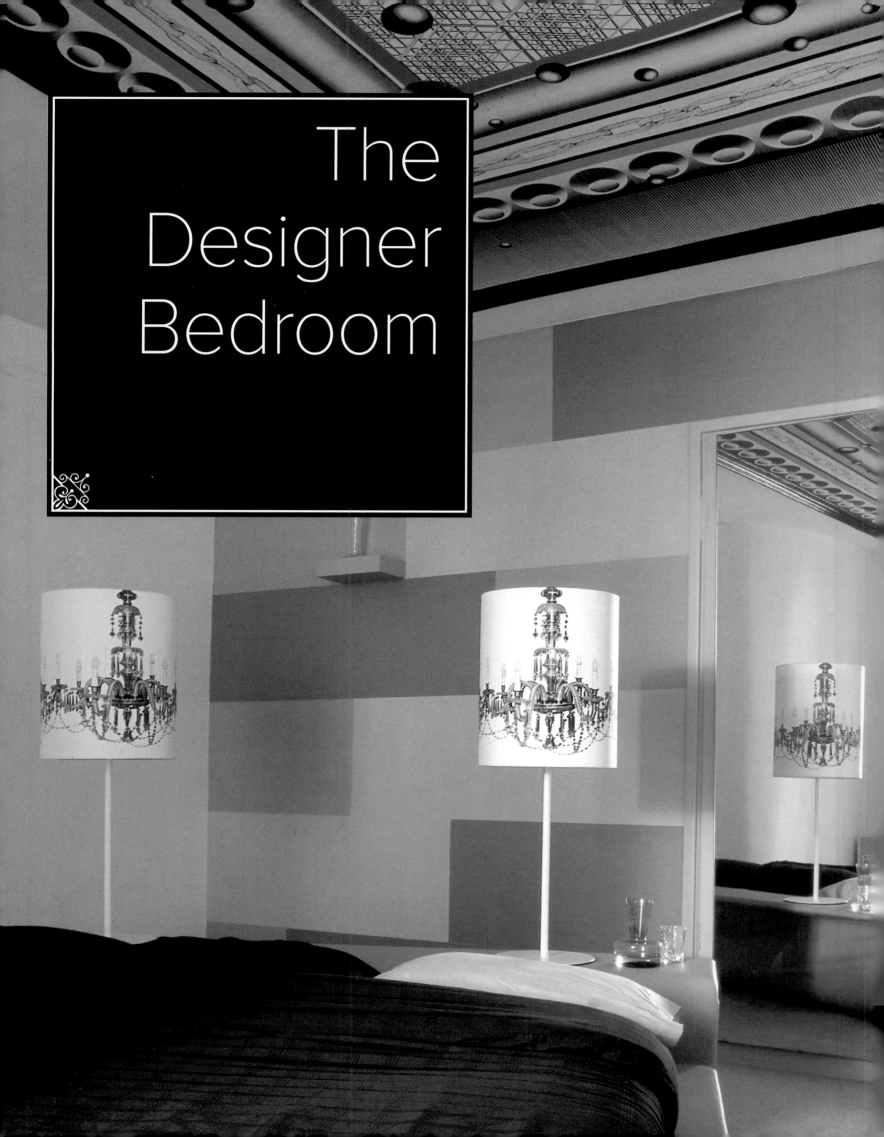

The Designer Bedroom

A potbellied chest of drawers, a voluminous period armoire, flowery wallpaper, and polished parquet—in postwar homes, distinctive decor was far from being the highest priority. After the chaos of war, Europe was more preoccupied with reconstruction than with style. Nevertheless, a few champions of interior design broke out of the mold to usher in a domestic revolution whose reverberations still resonate today.

In the 1950s, while Europe and many other parts of the world were beginning to follow the American model, accumulating refrigerators, vacuum cleaners, and washing machines, the visionary architect Le Corbusier unveiled his "Radiant City" housing development in Marseilles. Still, even here comfort and practicality took precedence over design per se.

In 1960, design made a dramatic entrance into the kitchen with Raymond Loewy's Coquelle saucepan, sold by Le Creuset. Then furniture created by Charlotte Perriand, Jean Prouvé, and Pierre Jeanneret captivated the new bourgeoisie, who already dreamed of clever storage spaces and comfortable sofas. Louis XV wing chairs were rapidly eclipsed by Italian, Scandinavian, and American furniture. The Western world, fascinated by the conquest of space, changed its style. In 1965, the ultra-contemporary red chairs of Olivier Mourgue made it into the space hotel in Stanley Kubrick's *2001: A Space Odyssey.* Color made an entrance into home design as new, more user-friendly modes of living came into vogue. Advances in technology were pressed into service to create objects at once useful and beautiful. Pierre Paulin, for example, was the first to pioneer modular furniture, lowering seats and covering steel frames with polyurethane foam.

But the real break with the past came in London, with the opening of Terence Conran's first Habitat store. Contemporary furniture and accessories both functional and fun were finally available to suit the rebellious generation of '68, who rejected the staid style of their parents' homes.

At the turn of the 1980s, the fascination with style brought about an increasing openness to influences from abroad, with fashion and interior design sharing many of the same influences. Andrée Putman initiated, at Morgans Hotel in New York, a minimalist aesthetic celebrating pure form and space while the Swedish superstore IKEA flooded the planet with affordable furniture, and Philippe Starck democratized design. At the beginning of the twenty-first century, designers who had parlayed their names into brands abounded, and consumers bought a designer label rather than a product or a style. Design had become the symbol of postmodern elegance.

At the same time, the popularity of modern design has been countered by a groundswell of nostalgia, with decorators like Jacques Garcia and Alberto Pinto revisiting the Baroque to magnificent effect.

Today, furniture is chosen not so much with an eye to convention as to reveal our own personality, and designers are the invaluable guides who show us how to express ourselves with style.

PREVIOUS SPREAD:

THE HAGUE

The artist-designer Ton of Holland makes ingenious use of handicraft. Her eighteenth-century residence, which she repaints every year, bears her personal stamp from floor to ceiling. Trompe-l'oeil, photocopies, découpage—anything can become fodder for her fantasy decor.

OPPOSITE:

SICILY

It is now possible to actually enter a work of art, thanks to patron of the arts Antonio Presti, whose Hotel Atelier sul Mare has art to suit all tastes. The disconcerting Sogni tra Segni bedroom is designed by Renato Curcio, an artist and former officer in the Red Brigade.

ABOVE:

PARIS

The interior architect Laurent Buttazzoni mixes unique artworks and factory-made objects, cultivating a severe asceticism leavened by a bit of kitsch. The Antony bed is by Jean Prouvé; the lamp is by Jasper Morisson. Near the mirror, a chair and a wall decoration by Verner Panton are juxtaposed with a bearskin rug on the oak floor. Finishing touches: lamps by Rizzatto, a zebu horn, and a Sony radio from the 1960s.

PREVIOUS SPREAD:

LONDON

The red velvet of the drapes and bed—which, like the side tables and lamps, is neoclassically inspired—glows with high drama against the white-painted floorboards. The sheepskin on a wooden chair from the Victorian era, carved in the startling shape of a bear, echoes the sheepskin rug and throw pillow and the fake fur bedspread. On the wall is an engraved heart-shaped Venetian mirror from the end of the nineteenth century.

LEFT:

PARIS

For designers Paul Mathieu and Michael Ray, "the bedroom is a room we guard jealously for ourselves." An immense nude against a bronze green background and heavy, deep green curtains transform this room into a distinctive, intensely intimate space.

OPPOSITE:

JODHPUR, INDIA

The palace of Umaid Bawan, the last to have been constructed in India, is one of the largest in the world, with 347 rooms. The Art Deco bedroom in the maharani's apartments is decorated with a fresco by Stefan Norblin that depicts the goddess Kali sitting astride a tiger.

OVERLEAF:

PARIS

In the guest room of Marc André Hubin's former apartment, set into a monumental lead shelving unit, an enormous gift, created by Gaetano Pesce, sits as a surprise for guests. A system of wires is used to lift the paper wrapping off the bed.

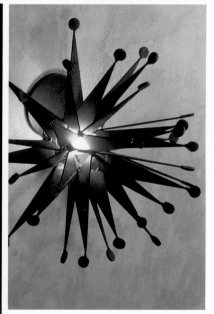

ABOVE AND LEFT:

MONACO

In the middle of Jean and Jessica Conrieri's bedroom stands an imposing architectural structure, a central iron column that screens the bed from view while also serving as a storage unit. This cabinet-bookshelf, a unique piece designed especially for this house by the designer Tom Dixon, was transported, with great difficulty, from London to Monaco. The supporting cast includes an eighteenth-century love seat, a candelabra by Francois Liguori, and a wall sconce by Tom Dixon.

OPPOSITE:

NEW YORK

In German fashion designer Wolfgang Joop's bedroom, a wood and steel screen created by American artist John Risley in 1957 serves as a headboard for the bed. A walnut bench by George Nakashima, Arne Jacobsen's Egg chair, and a wooden sculpture by Alexandre Noll complete the arrangement.

171

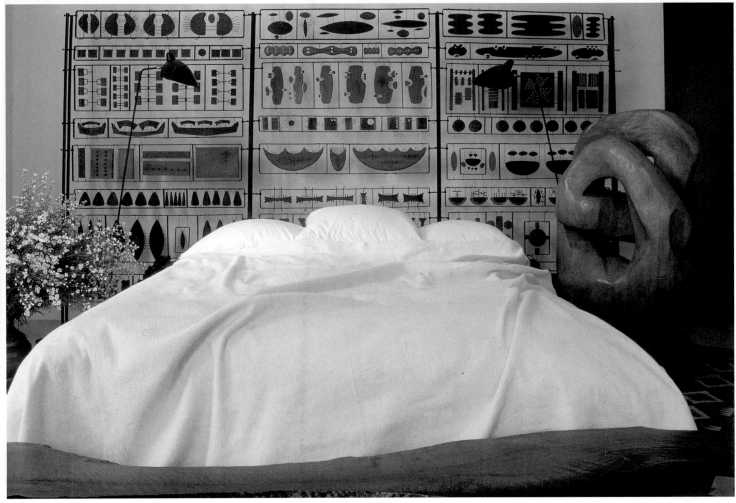

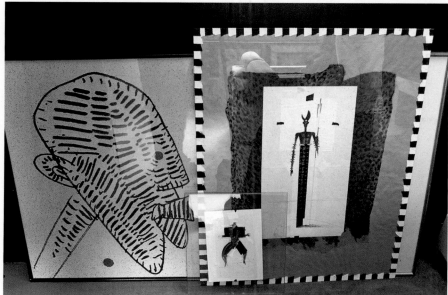

PARIS

In Jean-Paul Goude's Paris apartment, Andrée Putman
has created a bedroom nestled into a mahogany case.
"A real cigar box," Goude jokes. The wood gives the
room a very masculine touch, yet it also creates an
enveloping sensation, almost maternal and cocoonlike.
Storage and side tables are integrated into this
cabinet-room.

MILAN

Art lover and collector to the core, the couturier Gianfranco Ferre has been influenced by the paintings that aroused his first aesthetic impulses. The hot colors of Titian and Veronese, the classical sensuality of Fragonard, and the play of shadow and light of Cézanne are among the subtle references we can find in the home of the king of Italian elegance, notably in the mix of refined fabrics, furs, and precious woods.

OPPOSITE:

PARIS

The monochromatic bedroom of designer Christian Astuguevieille is an extended play on the essence of one material: hemp. Every piece in the room is covered in hemp rope. This sensual man sums up his approach: "In my civilization, one touches. One expresses oneself by smoothness, softness, the rugged, and the rough. I love used objects, objects that have been touched over and over, like fossils polished by the sea." The sober geometric alignment of the rope, in tightly wound patterns, is the mark of Astuguevieille's creative universe.

ABOVE AND LEFT:

LAUSANNE, SWITZERLAND

The distinctive style of Elisabeth Garouste and Mattia Bonetti, with its theatrical effects and recurrent wood motif, is recognizable in everything they touch. For Asher and Regina Edelman's bedroom, they created a bed that is romantic, poetic, and sensual, decorated with dreamlike branches of wrought iron.

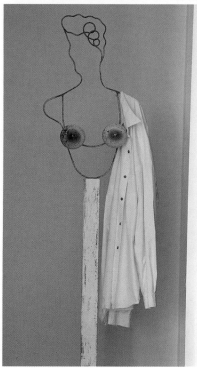

MIDI, FRANCE

In the south of France, interior architect Jacqueline Morabito has transformed the ruins of a shepherd's house into an immaculate little gem. Her work is the last word on the theme of white. The beauty of this bedroom lies in its extreme simplicity: a tinted cement floor, a Baroque relief serving as a headboard, narrow windows with linen shades.

RIGHT:

PARIS

Situated in a quintessentially Parisian hotel, this bedroom carries the stamp of elegance, at once rigorous and warm, of Andrée Putman. She combines subtlety, softness, and comfort without ostentation. Here, she has designed a curving screen of KoolShade bronze mesh, set in a frame of brushed steel.

OVERLEAF:

SAINT-SÉBASTIEN, SPAIN

For architect Gabriel Calparsoro, Andrée Putman has tucked the bed into an alcove lined with black-veined macassar ebony.

The Urban
Bedroom

PAGES 180-81:

LONDON

David Gill admits to a taste for spectacular forms. In the foreground, a sculpted polyester chair has been reupholstered in polyurethane faux leather.

PREVIOUS SPREAD:

LILLE, FRANCE

A careful selection of designer furniture—a bed and side tables by Carlo Colombo, and Shiro Kuramata's metal mesh Sing Sing Sing chair and black ash and chromed metal Ko-Ko occasional table—contribute to the clean-edged design of Thierry Laigle's apartment-gallery.

LEFT AND OPPOSITE:

NEW YORK

In an old factory loft acquired by Andy Katz, Bruce Banato has created a cube of a bathroom, open to the stamped-tin ceiling, with opaque glass panels set into two of the walls. Behind one of these, the bedroom benefits from the soft indirect light. In the bathroom are Corian basins and custom-made pivoting metal mirrors.

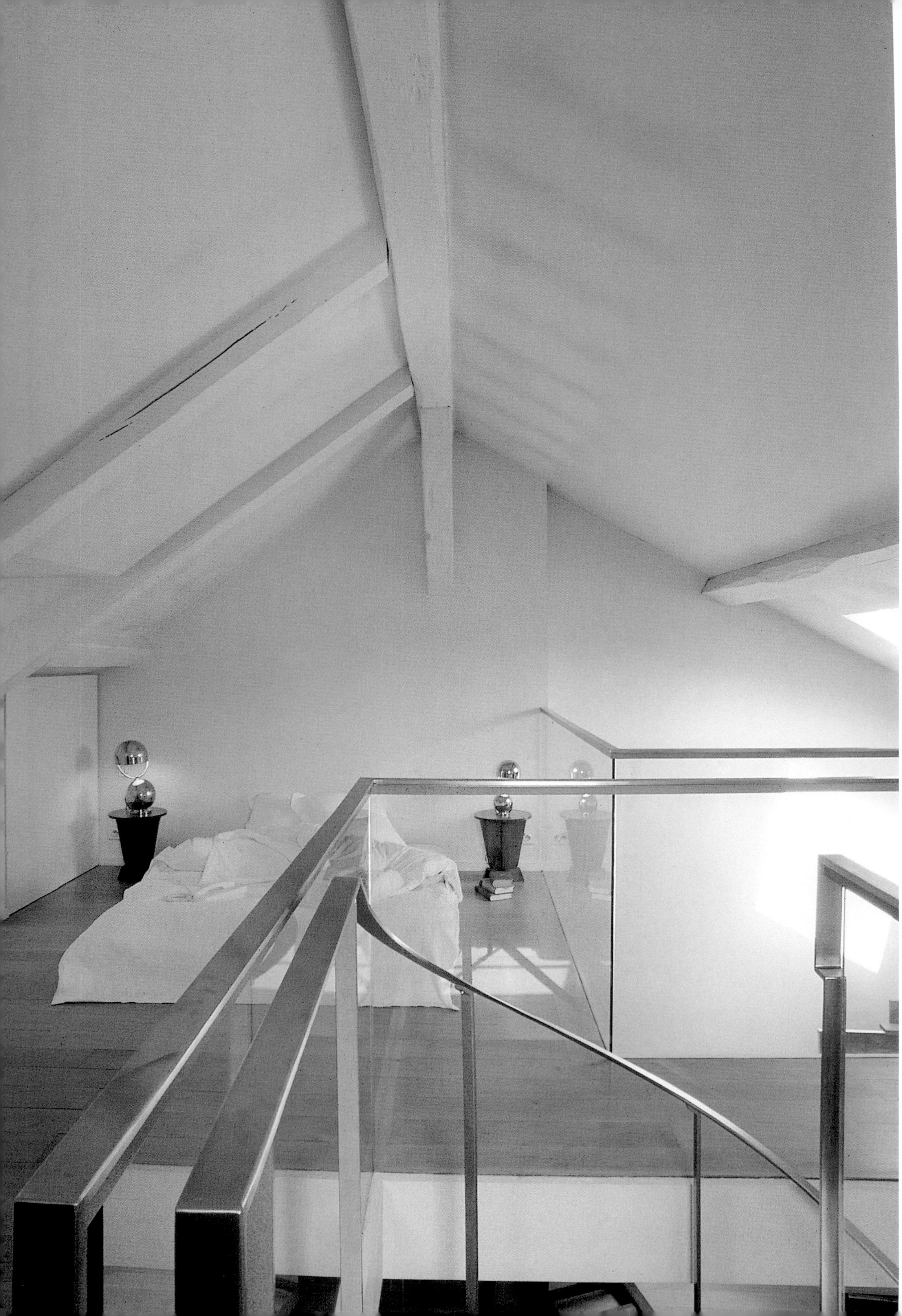

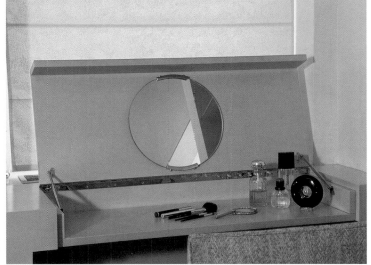

OPPOSITE:

PARIS

This spartan bedroom, designed by Andrée Putman for the painter Christophe von Weyhe, is reached by way of an epoxy staircase with a banister of matte nickel-plated metal. Art Deco bedside tables flank the bed.

ABOVE:

NEW YORK

In the Metropolitan Tower, a New York skyscraper, Andrée Putman has renovated a luxury apartment. The bedside table is a reedition by Pierre Chareau, and the painting is by Barry Le Va. The pale sycamore vanity shelf built into the wall was designed by Putman.

JOHANNESBURG

The interior decorator Laurie Owen has emphasized
natural, soothing materials and colors in this bedroom.
The cotton- and velour-covered bed sits on thick
whitewashed boards of linden wood. Sheepskins
scattered on the white cement floor accentuate the
soft atmosphere.

ABOVE:

ANVERS, BELGIUM

This fluid and harmonious room, designed by architect Marc Corbiau, is paneled with planks of pickled and sanded cedar. The floor is sycamore; the chair and lamps are by Christian Liaigre; and the ceiling fan's blades are fashioned from fabric in a frame of curved fishing rods.

OVERLEAF:

SHANGHAI

For the gallery owner Pearl Lam, Andrée Putman has created a bedroom with a bath in an extension; the panels slide shut when necessary. The wall unit that serves as a headboard conceals a number of secret compartments of different sizes.

TOP:

SIEM REAP, CAMBODIA

In this subtly decorated and refined bedroom in the FCC Angkor hotel—which was built on the site of the old French governor's residence—the bath is hidden behind sliding panels.

BOTTOM:

SIEM REAP, CAMBODIA

This ancient villa of King Sihanouk is now the exceptional Amansara Hotel, where quiet elegance reigns. Dark wood paneling is set off by ivory walls and a floor in pale gray terrazzo.

OPPOSITE:

PARIS

In the calm and sensual bedroom Laurent Buttazoni designed for Katy Barker, two mirrors face each other. One functions as the bed's headboard; the other, in a 1940s frame, serves to visually enlarge the space.

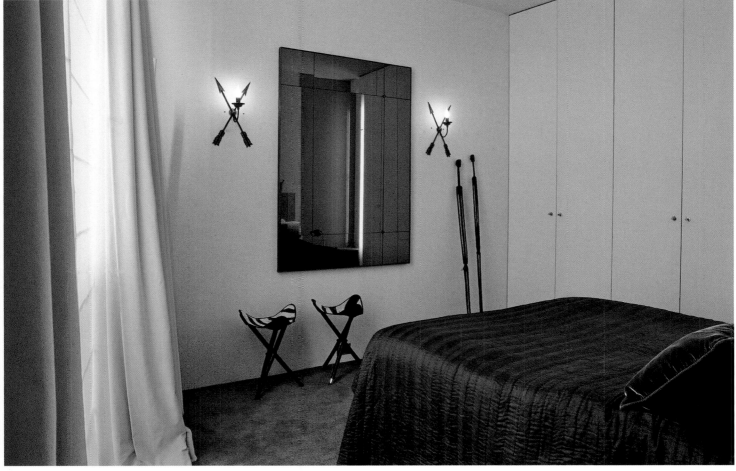

PARIS

A bedroom and bath
created by Christian Duc,
separated by a narrow
counter topped with a
mirror.

PARIS

This arrangement by interior designer Michel Boyer encourages free circulation
between the bedroom and the bath, hidden behind a sliding panel framed in dark-
stained oak. On the left, Tom Dixon's sinuous S chair of rush over a steel framework.

LEFT AND ABOVE:

BERLIN

This study-bedroom, created in an old factory loft by architecture and interior design firm Peanutz Architekten, holds many surprises. The bookshelves, in imitation mahogany, slide away to reveal a built-in bath.

OVERLEAF:

LONDON

A decor of minimal purity characterizes this serene bedroom designed by Philippe Starck for the Hotel Sanderson.

After the long reign of the subtle and the neutral, color has again surfaced in the house. While it would have been unthinkable only ten years ago to paint a bedroom wall the color of raspberry puree, today it is quite common. And it seems that this freedom in wall color has only followed the trend set by other design elements.

Furniture was first to break away from the monopoly of black, white, and gray in the 1980s and 90s, which itself came about in part as a reaction against the color explosion of the hippies.

Once again, times have changed, and color has returned little by little to residences—an orange pouffe, a red chest of drawers. . . Cognoscenti early on advocated color to a large public. Their first goal was to seduce a young clientele, whose use of bright hues would then bring about a wider change. Artistic tableware and stylish kitchen gadgets made early inroads, with dishes in vivid colors and small electric appliances clothed in acid or pastel hues.

Once, there were certain ranges of colors associated with each stage in life. Of course, where a person lived also had to be taken into account, since the tastes of a city dweller differ from those of country residents.

At first there were the standard shades of paint—beige, and the eggshell white that suggested brightness, calm, and a clean look. Today, however, even those people who want light hues dismiss these ordinary shades as uninspired, choosing instead the natural tones of linen, hemp, and raffia. These colors also blend harmoniously with the more eco-friendly furniture now in vogue. Nature's an inexhaustible source of inspiration: the greens of leaves, tea, or bamboo warm earth and clay tones; the blues and greens of the sea, with its pale foam, are all much in demand.

Still in the family of muted colors, another range of shades has emerged recently: those inspired by minerals. Some of these colors are matt and dull; some seem almost metallic. Gray, formerly confined to industrial buildings, and the colors of stone and pebbles have now entered into every room of the house, notably the bedroom.

Finally, the most striking tendency the last few years has been toward humor and kitsch—sparkling, very Bollywood. Visible everywhere, this audacious use of color is gaining more and more devotees. Peony red, fuchsia, guava, turquoise, violet, and acid green all make a pleasant surprise. Intense colors flaunt themselves glowing for all to see in every room, and the bedroom has hardly escaped from this phenomenon. The craziest, most audacious colors are now fair game, whether on floors, walls, furniture, or woodwork.

PREVIOUS SPREAD, LEFT, AND OPPOSITE:

THÉOULE-SUR-MER, FRANCE

The house of couturier Pierre Cardin is an extraordinary monument to 1960s architecture. Designed by visionary architect Antti Lovag, this labyrinthine residence, all in curves, uses an astounding palette of colors.

MELBOURNE

For architects Kai Chen and Ian Robinson, color is an integral part of the structure of the house. In the bedroom, the north wall is painted violet, as if lost in the shadows. In effect, their theme for this project is "color in the shadows." Most of the colors used are saturated hues, deliberately deepened to allow the shadows to creep in.

SICILY

Antonio Presti, proprietor of the Hotel
Atelier sul Mare and promoter of a series
of artistic initiatives, has asked renowned
international artists to design fifteen of the
hotel's forty rooms. In the space of ten years,
he has successfully transformed an area far
removed from the tourist circuit into a place
of discovery for those passionate about
art. Above, the triangular Tinacria bedroom
designed by Mauro Staccioli, with its sharp-
angled bed and deeply tinted cement walls.

MARRAKECH

In this bedroom in Franca and Carla Sozzani's *riad,* or guest house, the design
is conceived by Kris Ruh, an American artist who lives in Marrakech and Italy.
His composition—walls tinted with a patina of violet blue, a pierced-metal lamp,
elaborate ironwork, and Indian textiles—is set off by *zelliges,* the tile mosaics used for
the floor and the stair risers.

CAPE TOWN

In the blue bedroom of the South African fashion designer Malcom Kluk, a niche in the wall becomes a bookshelf. The books are cleverly placed with their spines inward to create a striking graphic tableau.

LEFT AND OPPOSITE,
TOP LEFT:

LONDON

For his bedroom, the
fashion designer Matthew
Williamson initially imag-
ined an exotic Oriental
space in deep magenta
and violet. A coat of white
paint later, a fluorescent
pink has seized possession
of the room, along with
Asian mural paintings.

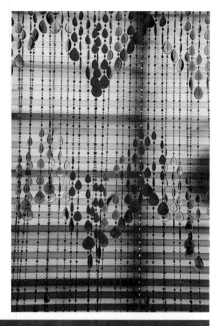

TOP RIGHT AND BOTTOM:

JOHANNESBURG

In Marianne Fassler's bedroom, eclecticism rules the day, with "girlie" pink walls and traditional mats on the floor. A chair reupholstered in fake leopardskin echoes the leopard print on the bed.

ABOVE:

GOA, INDIA

Ari Ajwani and Claudia Derain have decorated their "alternative" hotel, Le Nilaya, by using color with abandonment and by mixing Indian and occidental influences.

LEFT:

JAIPUR, INDIA

For Marie-Hélène de Taillac, color reigns supreme, notably pink, the euphoric color par excel ence.

OPPOSITE:

PROVENCE

The deep red of Daniel Vial's bedroom was inspired by the baked clay of the south of France. The bed is set on a straw mat; beside it stands an earthenware jar and a lantern that evokes Morocco. Hanging from the gunpowder gray window frame, a bright tasseled cord completes the simple, cheerful decor.

NEW DELHI

Manish Arora is a fashion designer and one of the great
hopes of the Indian subcontinent, having garnered
considerable success in Europe. His source of inspiration is India, a land that still offers a breath of innovation
and originality, making its mark throughout the
trendy Western world. Here Indian vibrations infuse a
multicolor bedroom that brings together a four-poster
and snazzy visuals—the over-the-top spirit of Bollywood
is not far off!

MIDI, FRANCE

There are no bad colors, only bad matches. This is the reason that color fascinates
and intimidates at the same time. At his home, painter Hervé Thibault has a knack
for assembling delicate colors to create a world of great visual pleasure.

LUXOR, EGYPT

Some civilizations,
like the Nubian, have
always known how to
handle color.

TOP LEFT AND BOTTOM:

CAPE TOWN

In Malcolm Kluk's former house, an eclectic mix of styles—antiques sit next to simple pieces of furniture, and photos glued directly to the wall face antique frames—gives this bedroom a comfortable, informal atmosphere.

TOP RIGHT:

BALI

Emerald green creates an enchanting entrance.

Whether inspired by Oriental, Asian, or African style, the bedroom is without doubt the most intimate room in the house; it reveals, often in spite of ourselves, our tastes, our interests, and our lifestyle.

It is also the room where we can allow ourselves to experiment with urges and fantasies, and let our personality make an impression on our own space . . . so private. The essential thing is to create our own sense of well-being.

Why not take inspiration from bedrooms from remote corners of the planet, then, and profit from the lore and know-how of age-old civilizations?

India's palaces, for example, attest to the refinement and splendor of the maharajas surrounded by their courts, balanced between public and private life. Marble, gems, paintings, precious woods and fabrics, grand spaces . . . all the ingredients for an enchanted atmosphere are there. And don't forget that for the majority of Hindus, every small daily task is tied to a god or goddess, and the bedroom is often not only a place to sleep but also a sacred area that protects the defenseless sleeper from the dangers of the outside world. In the Indian home, built of masonry or mud brick, there is a distinction between the veranda or parlor where one receives visitors, the kitchen, and the room reserved only for family members. The *carpai,* or traditional bed, with a wood frame strung with rope or woven strips of cotton, is ubiquitous throughout all of India.

In Indonesia, the enchantment derives above all from a sublime simplicity. The Indonesian bedroom possesses an elegance devoid of artifice, a simplicity accentuated by the asceticism of the bed. Pure harmony as a source of inspiration, inviting meditation and perhaps wisdom—it all conveys a delicate atmosphere, combining asceticism and relaxation.

The style of the African bedroom derives from a mix of artisanal traditions and history. The room's details reveal a sense of authenticity hard to find in other countries. Rather than simply flat panels, the walls are fertile fields for express on that can be prepared like a canvas. Smoothed and sanded, they become supple supports for a variety of colors and designs of incomparable beauty. The bed is a dais on which a mat is laid at night; during the day, food containers are set on it. It is not considered an object of absolute necessity like weapons, farm tools, and kitchen utensils.

In Zanzibar, traditional mats are used everywhere in the "green" buildings on Mnemba Island.

In the Maghreb, a continuous exchange of people, culture, and commodities with Spain since the eleventh century has given the place an extremely rich culture, especially in Morocco. The joyous architecture of the medinas also bears witness to this double origin: multicolored earthenware mosaics on the floor and walls, chiseled stucco decorations, and painted or sculpted wooden ceilings.

223

PREVIOUS SPREAD:

GARB ASWAN, EGYPT

An exterior view of the Nubian dwellings of southern Egypt.

OPPOSITE, TOP, AND LEFT:

GARB ASWAN, EGYPT

In Nubian houses, collections of cooking vessels, brilliantly painted motifs, and colorful woven palm-leaf and papyrus baskets hung on the walls are decorations in their own right.

ABOVE:

OUALATA, MAURETANIA

In this multifunctional bedroom, niches used as shelves are surrounded by splendid red-brown trompe l'oeil designs.

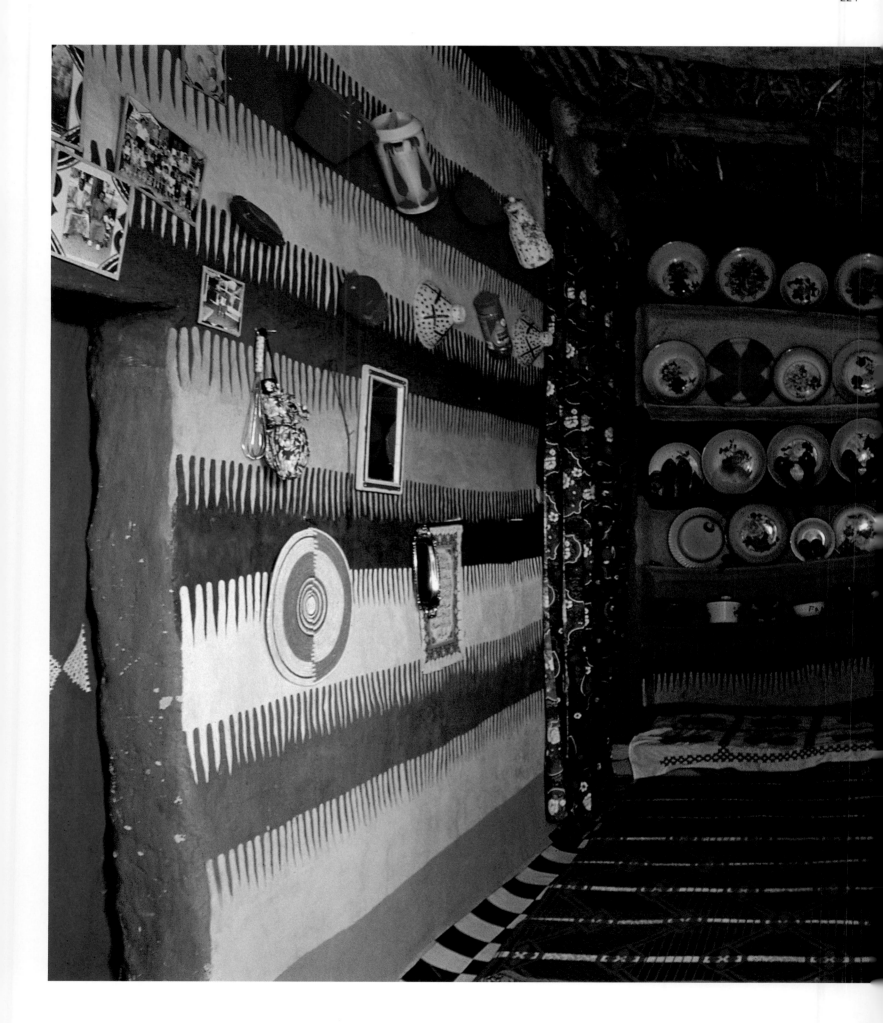

MAURETANIA, NEAR SELIBABI

Rich colors cover these walls in ancestral geometrical patterns that are still used today to decorate interiors. All of this ornamentation has a meaning, symbolizing the enduring bond between man and nature. In the past, women used natural pigments and mud to make these designs; today they have longer-lasting man-made paints at their disposal. The zigzags are not only very decorative but modify our perception of the space; the absence of furniture amplifies their impact.

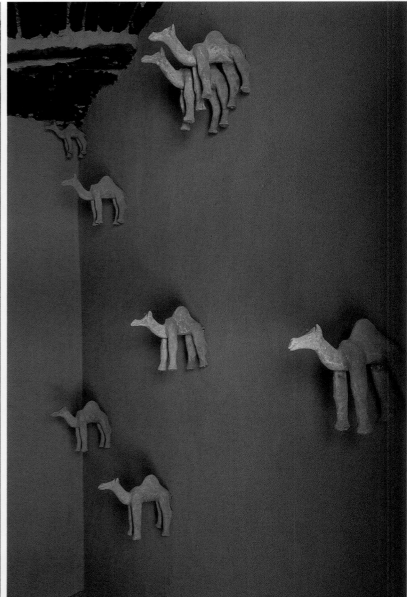

AGADEZ, NIGER

At the home of artist Not Vital, the roofline is punctuated with cattle horns. Another emblematic animal, the camel, used as a mount or a beast of burden in the deserts of Africa and Arabia, projects from the bedroom walls in high relief. These "ships of the desert" seem to come alive as a subtle play of shadows and light caresses the velvet-smooth earthen walls.

AGADEZ, NIGER

In Africa, some traditional ceilings are composed of wooden sticks used as joists. Above, a dense layer of branches, held together with a mixture of damp earth, lime, sand, straw, and ash, create an impermeable barrier. Not Vital's house shows some beautiful examples of this kind of ceiling.

GOUROUNSI COUNTRY, BURKINA FASO

The wall paintings of the Kassenas women are extremely varied in their design; a V shape, as here, signifies welcome. For these murals, the women use volcanic rock, found near the village, which they pound into red, black, and brown powders. The geometrical motifs used can vary from one village to another, and sometimes from one house to the next. In general, the decoration of these mud-walled houses is reserved for the most creative women.

THE HIGH ATLAS, MOROCCO

Thick sheared-wool rugs in various sizes, decorated
with simple or complex designs, completely cover the
entire interior. Their warm, vibrant colors enliven even
the most rudimentary of Moroccan houses. Designed
to keep out the cold, these thick rugs also serve as beds,
while modern metallic gold emergency blankets are
sometimes used for their decorative effect.

DJABOUL, SYRIA

Under the domed roofs of these homes, woodstoves serve as symbols of success. In a room that serves as a living room in the day and a bedroom at night, they occupy a central place. Here, tea is heated, to be sipped while resting on cushions placed on the floor.

MANDAWA, INDIA

After Kesri Singh inherited an eighteenth-century fort, he converted it to a hotel. With the architects Vasant and Revathi Kamath, passionate devotees of earthenware architecture, he also created the Mandawa Desert Camp in the nearby sand dunes. The mud-brick houses in the neighboring villages served as a wonderful source of inspiration, notably in their use of mica, a glittering mineral incorporated into the walls.

TOP AND BOTTOM LEFT:

GUJARAT, INDIA

In the huts of the Rabaris, a nomadic tribe in the Thar Desert, women make storage units out of clay into which is set mica, small mirrors, and fragments of colored glass. Stacks of colorful patchwork blankets are suspended from the ceiling, to be unfolded at night to cover the rammed-earth floor.

BOTTOM RIGHT:

ORISSA, INDIA

On the interior as well as exterior, mud walls are covered in a profusion of hand-painted designs. The pyramid motifs here, delineated with rice paste, evoke mounds of newly harvested rice and suggest abundance, fertility, and prosperity.

PONDICHERRY, INDIA

On the coast of Coromandel, on a thirty-acre site bordering the beach, Dimitri Klein has conceived the Dune Hotel as an artists' retreat. For two years, he has welcomed artists, who have contributed their artworks (paintings, sculptures, lamps) to bungalows while they were being built. The result: about thirty eclectic, sometimes even a bit startling, houses.

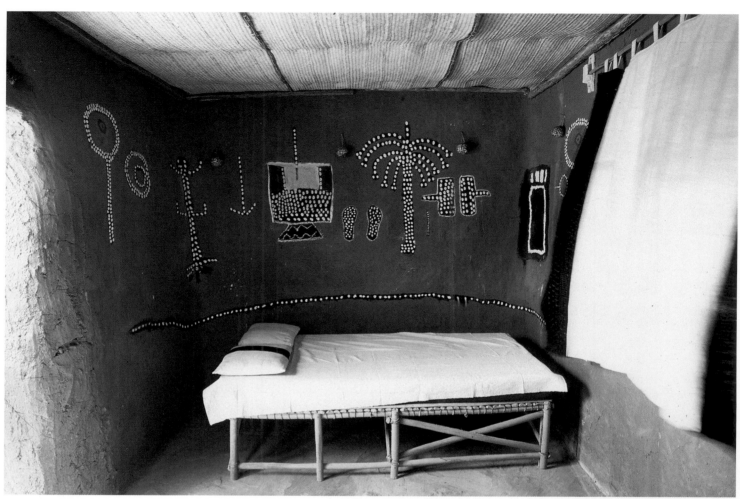

DOGON COUNTRY, MALI

At the settlement of Aly Guindo, near Biandagara, traditional mud-brick construction is an omnipresent resource that encourages an exceptionally creative architecture. The inlay and murals were created by local artists.

MOYO ISLAND, INDONESIA

In Asia, vegetative materials have always been preferred to masonry for building. Thus, floors might be made of reeds laid side by side, which promote good air circulation and the dissipation of humidity. The exterior walls are constructed out of screens of loosely woven bamboo. In the past this method of building allowed houses to be quickly packed up and moved out of the way of marauders, or even to be sold independently of the land they were built on.

ABOVE:

MNEMBA ISLAND, ZANZIBAR, TANZANIA

Bandas are the original sustainable housing, built exclusively with natural materials, including an impressive number of straw mats. These locally produced mats are ubiquitous here, used on the floor, the walls, and the front veranda.

OPPOSITE TOP:

BANGKOK

Nagara Sambandaraska's home is composed of many individual teak pavilions: pavilions for relaxing or sleeping, a music salon, a library-office, and—the most impressive—for entertaining guests. Each pavilion, decorated with a refined touch, harmoniously blends contemporary art and precious antiques.

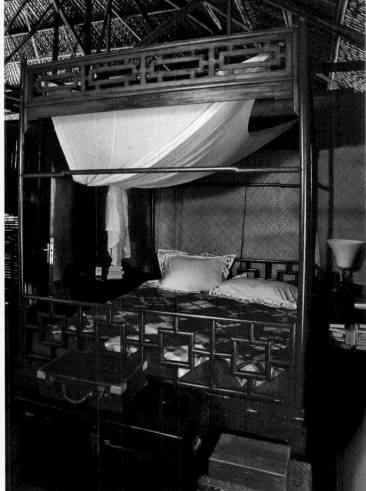

ABOVE:

NAIROBI

In the savannah, a large modern mud-walled residence houses the traditional African art collection of Alan Donovan, head of African Heritage, a society dedicated to promoting African culture.

ABOVE:

SAIGON

In one of the bedrooms of this house by Thien Nga Schwab, the geometric lines of a canopied bed of Chinese inspiration play off those of the beams supporting a roof thatched in *nipa,* an aquatic coconut palm. The walls, which do not come all the way up to the roof, as is often the case in tropical residences, are made of palm-fiber mats.

MULBEKH, LADAKH, INDIA

In the foothills of the Himalayas, the houses are
constructed of stone and wood, with thick walls and
very small openings, to conserve heat when the
temperature drops to -20°F. At night, this reception
room, richly decorated with Buddhist symbols,
transforms into a cozy bedroom.

LEFT AND ABOVE:

RAJASTHAN, INDIA

The fortified palace of Deogarh Mahal
was the residence of the *rawats* (princes)
of Deogarh, who reigned over an area
consisting of about 210 villages. The
bedrooms, each one rivaling the next in
beauty and refinement, are decorated with
delicate frescoes depicting both epic tales
and scenes of daily life.

OVERLEAF:

OUTSKIRTS OF JODHPUR,
RAJASTHAN, INDIA

Raghavendra Rathore and his brother have
been steadily working on restoring the little
fort of Narlai, once a hunting lodge for the
maharajas of Jodhpur. The walls of the oldest
bedrooms are covered with a richly painted
stucco called *airaish*.

The Outdoor Bedroom

Ah, siesta! The sweet respite of a refreshing after-lunch nap is not reserved only for layabouts. Vehemently advocated by their devotees, naps might even be considered a necessity, inscribed as they are in our evolutionary blueprint. The civilizations that have subscribed to this view over the centuries have understood it well: among the extraordinary variety of ancient Roman beds, for example (for conversation in salons, for reading in the library, and so on), were those dedicated to daytime rest. These enthusiasts of the nap would go as far as to invite their friends along to keep them company. Even today, in Mexico, the whole country takes a siesta after the midday meal, and in China this break in the day is officially prescribed, stipulated in their constitution since 1949.

Although this custom properly belongs to the world's warmer regions, where afternoon heat makes any exertion difficult, northern countries have recently taken to it with delight.

What is better than a siesta? André Gide admitted to allowing himself two hours a day, sometimes more, and enjoyed it immensely. A third of France admits to being fervent supporters of the idea, including many overbooked businessmen, artists, and politicians. Unofficially, of course!

True, the siesta suffers from an image of sloth, and seems incompatible with the demands of modern Western society. Even in the countries where it is still a tradition, such as Spain, the time allotted for the midday rest is diminishing little by little. However, it has been scientifically proven that this brief instant of separation from the stresses of the world—twenty minutes is plenty—is very beneficial, restoring our strength, focus, and effectiveness. The lesson is, we lose some time to gain it. To dream with wide open eyes, then, we invite you to skim through this photo essay in praise of the siesta under the open sky.

PREVIOUS SPREAD:

MARRAKECH

To soften the glare of the sunlight, the architect Quentin Wilbaux designed shades of heavy canvas, pierced with grommets and suspended from wooden poles.

ABOVE:

LAMU, TANZANIA

At the end of the day, enchanting little lamps sparkle on the roof terrace of Anita Spoerri's house.

ABOVE:

MARRAKECH

As the shades of night descend, lanterns throw off a soft and flattering light. It is impossible to resist the magic of these glass and pierced-metal lanterns.

OVERLEAF:

MARRAKECH

A multitude of rugs and outdoor beds made of blocks of foam covered in cotton decorate the flat roof of Meryanne Loum-Martin's *riad,* with its view out over the palm groves.

LEFT:

TOKYO

On the terrace of British fashion designer Nigel Curtiss's home, a double hammock is suspended from the roof beams for siestas with a view of the deck, the pool, and, farther off, the sea.

ABOVE:

BRITTANY AND NORMANDY

The hammock is essential for reading, sleeping, dreaming, or sharing privileged moments of intimacy, on a porch or under a tree.

ZANZIBAR

On Mnemba Island, accessible only by boat, you can discover the pleasure of living the life of Robinson Crusoe deluxe. On this tiny piece of land, which you can cover on foot in twenty minutes, there are no roads and no automobiles of any kind. The ten bungalows, constructed of palm and banana mats on a beach of sparkling sand, were decorated by Chris Brown. Siesta is taken in the shade of "walking palm" (*Pandanus rabaiensis*), a strange plant that props itself up on aboveground roots as if tiptoeing across the sand.

ZANZIBAR

A magical atmosphere suffused with Omani and
African influences colors the island of Zanzibar. On the
terrace that opens out onto the Indian ocean, Sylvia
and Torgeir Vaage have installed a small lounging area
with daybeds to soak up the sun, sip ginger juice, or
dine with friends.

DAR TAMSNA, MARRAKECH

A succession of ogival arches made of unfired clay bricks, coated with ocher *tadelakt* (lime plaster), create this veranda. The floor of *bejmate,* or hand-made fired bricks, is covered with Turkish and Moroccan kilims. The furniture, crafted by local artisans, is upholstered with cotton hand-woven in Senegal.

ABOVE:

MIDI, FRANCE

Dappled light filters through vines in this pleasant, drowsy space created by interior designer Agnès Comar.

TOP:

MALINDI, KENYA

A blend of classicism and primitivism characterizes the work of Amando Tanzini in this East African dwelling, with its monumentally columned veranda.

BOTTOM:

UBUD, BALI

Anneka van Waesberghe's terrace can be closed up with simple bamboo blinds. The chaise longues and teak benches furnished with white cotton cushions invite idle hours.

TOP:

RAJASTHAN, INDIA

In the Hotel Aman-I-Khas, the suites designed by Franco-Belgian decorator Jean-Michel Gathy have no partitions and are open to the outdoors.

BOTTOM:

GALLE, SRI LANKA

Everything here evokes the colonial period—the architecture, the caned daybeds, the monumental columns. Long cotton drapes protect loungers from harsh sun.

262

PREVIOUS SPREAD:

PONDICHERRY, INDIA

At the Dune Hotel, an open-air lounge under a thatched roof is only a few steps from the beach.

OPPOSITE, ABOVE, AND RIGHT:

UBUD, BALI

The teak, thatch-roofed house of Anneke van Waesberghe is open to nature. The openings are not fitted with windows, which are unnecessary in this tropical climate. Upstairs, on a terrace suspended over frangipani trees, two benches that serve as sofas during the day can be put together to make a bed at night.

OPPOSITE:

NORTH ISLAND, SEYCHELLES

In a small private lounge next to a circular pool, it is
pleasant to close your eyes and dream, or open them
to admire the sublime countryside. These structures,
directly inspired by nature, were created by architects
Lesley Carstens and Silvio Rech.

ABOVE:

MOMBO, BOTSWANA

These safari camps are gems of sustainable architecture. Made of wood and weather-resistant coated
fabric, these structures by South African architect
Silvio Rech nestle under majestic trees. Mounted on
stilts, each bedroom is linked to the next by a wooden
walkway. On the terrace, guests can relax and observe
the wildlife of the Okavango delta.

OVERLEAF:

CORSICA

A spacious deck of cedar turned a silvery gray by the
marine air faces out over the Mediterranean Sea and
the small port down below. This house, built by architect
Gilles Bouchez, has allied itself with the march of time,
suggesting a modern way to live in the summer.

RESOURCES

ARTELANO
Contemporary furniture.
54, rue de Bourgogne
75007, Paris
Tel. +33.1.44.18.00.00
www.artelano.com

ATELIER D'OFFARD
François-Xavier Richard's beautiful hand block-printed wallpaper made with natural pigments. Collections include ancient prints, Jacques-Émile Ruhlmann reprints, and contemporary creations.
9, rue Anatole France
37300 Joué-les-Tours, France
Tel. +33.2.47.67.93.22

BATHSHOP
tiling, furniture, and home accessories for chic and high-tech bathrooms.
3, rue Gros
75016 Paris
Tel. +33.1.46.47.50.58
www.bathshop.fr

CLIPSO DESIGN
Wall and ceiling coverings, lighting features, fine art mounting options, visual merchandising solutions, and special event displays.
9 route d'Englisberg
1763 Granges Paccot Switzerland
Tel. +41.2.64.60.55.88
www.clipso-design.com
www.clipso.ch/
United States Office:
395 Jordan Road
Sedona, AZ 86336
Tel. +1.928.282.4880
www.clipso-usa.com

COMPACTCONCRETE.COM
Francesco Passaniti brings concrete to life for interior design, applied arts, and sculpture. Design and manufacture of furniture and objects. Bathtubs, stools, pedestal tables, shelves, wall panels in a vast array of colors and finishes.
Francesco Passaniti atelier
22, passage Bourdeau
94200 Ivry-sur-Seine, France
Tel. +33.1.46.71.90.88

THE CONRAN SHOP
Furniture and home design.
New York:
The Conran Shop Bridgemarket
407 E. 59th Street
New York, NY 10022
Tel. +1.866.755.9079
www.conranusa.com
London:
The Conran Shop Chelsea
Michelin House
81 Fulham Road
London SW3 6RD
Tel. +44.20.7589.7401
www.conranshop.co.uk
Tokyo:
Living Design Centre, Ozone
Shinjuku Park Tower 3-4F
3-7-1 Nishi-Shinjuku
Tokyo 163-1062
Tel. +81.3.5322.6600

COULEURS INTÉRIEURES
Eco paint, pigments, and paintbrushes.
3, rue d'Angleterre
59000 Lille, France
Tel. +33.3.20.39.12.61

CRUCIAL TRADING
Natural floor coverings and custom-made rugs in sisal, seagrass, jute, and coir.
79 Westbourne Park Road
London W2 5QH
Tel. +44.20.7221.9000
The Plaza
535 King's Road
London SW10 0SZ
Tel. +44.20.7376.7100

DESIGNERS GUILD
Fabric and wallpaper collections, furniture, bed and bath, paint, and luxury home accessories. Owned by Tricia Guild and Simon Jeffreys.
Head Office:
3 Latimer Place
London W10 6QT
Tel. +44.20.7893.7400
www.designersguild.com
United States Contacts:
Designers Guild Bed & Bath USA
Tel. +1.800.303.5413 (Customer Service)
Designers Guild Fabric & Wallpaper
(distributed by Osborne & Little)
Tel. +1.203.359.1500
Showroom (Trade Only):
7 W. 34th Street
New York, NY 10001
Tel. +1.212.967.4540
www.designersguildus.com

DIAGONALE
Flooring, tiling, and bathroom design.
4, rue Saint Sabin
750011 Paris
Tel. +33.1.47.00.80.33
www.diagonaledesign.net

DIX HEURES DIX
Lamp design.
Erdre Active
5, rue de la Toscane - B.P. 4308 - 44243
La Chapelle sur Erdre Cedex, France
Tel. +33.2.40.99.85.00.
www.dixheuresdix.com

ÉLITIS
Wall coverings, fabrics, and furniture.
35, rue de Bellechasse
75007 Paris
Tel. +33.1.45.51.51.00
www.elitis.fr

EMERY & CIE
*Paints, fine cloth, furniture, fabrics, rugs,
tableware, tiles, lighting, ironmongery, and
wallpaper.*
18, passage de la Main d'Or
75011 Paris
Tel. +33.1.44.87.02.02
www.emeryetcie.com

FARROW & BALL
Traditional wallpapers and paint.
Postal Address:
1054 Yonge Street
Toronto, ON M4W 2L1
Tel. +1.416.920.0200
Showrooms:
D & D Building
979 Third Avenue, Suite 1519
New York, NY 10022
Tel. +1.212.752.5544
249 Fulham Road
London SW3 6HY
Tel. +44.20.7351.0273

HABITAT
*Beds, bed linens, curtains, bookcases, and
contemporary lamps.*
Registered Office:
42–46 Princelet Street
London E1 5LP
Tel. +44.87.0411.5501
www.habitat.net

HOULÈS
*Trimmings, curtain poles, furnishing fabrics,
and accessories for curtains.*
18, rue Saint-Nicolas
75012 Paris
Tel. +33.1.43.44.65.19
www.houles.com

IDZIF
*Nature, travel, and pop-art themed
decorative stickers of various sizes and colors.*
45, rue Delizy
93500 Pantin, France
Tel. +33.1.41.83.32.32
www.idzif.fr

IN CRÉATION
*Personalized wall coverings designed by
young and talented artists.*
19, rue Pasteur
75011 Paris
Tel. +33.1.49.29.09.45
www.increation-online.com

J. PANSU
*Decorative fabrics, household accessories,
rugs, and Halluin tapestries.*
42, rue du Faubourg-Poissonnière
75010 Paris
Tel. +33.1.42.46.72.45
www.pansu.com

KÄHRS
*A vast array of wooden flooring and surface
treatments.*
Global Contact:
AB Gustaf Kähr Box 804,
SE-382 38 Nybro, Sweden
Tel. +46.481.460.00
www.kahrs.com

KENZO
*Upscale furniture coverings and home
accessories.*
Sold at Lelièvre:
13, rue du Mail
75002 Paris
Tel. +33.1.43.16.88.00
www.kenzo.com, www.lelievre.eu

KVADRAT
*High-quality modern textiles and textile-
related products.*
Headquarters:
Lundbergsvej 10
8400 Ebeltoft, Denmark
London Showroom:
62, Princedale Road
London W11 4NL
Tel. +44.20.7229.9969
New York Showroom:
Maharam
251 Park Avenue South
New York, NY 10010
Tel. +1.800.645.3943
www.kvadrat.dk

**LE CÈDRE ROUGE DU
PRINCE JARDINIER**
Outdoor teak furniture.
46, rue du Bac
75007 Paris
Tel. +33.1.44.55.07.15
www.princejardinier.fr

LELIÈVRE
Fine furnishing fabrics.
Lelièvre UK Ltd:
108–110 Chelsea Harbour Design Center
London SW10 0XE
Tel. +44.20.7352.4798
Stark Carpet/Old World Weavers:
979 Third Avenue, 11th floor
New York, NY 10022
Mercer House Interiors Ltd:
19-27 Wyndham Street
G/F Wilson House
Central Hong Kong
Tel. +852.2524.2000
www.lelievre.eu

LIGNE ROSET
Quality contemporary furnishings.
Roset USA Corp.:
Trinity Center
111 Broadway, Suite 1004
New York, NY 10006
Tel. +1.212.358.9204
Tel. +1.800.BY.ROSET
Roset (UK) Ltd:
Overcroft House
Badminton Court
Church Street, Amersham
Bucks HP7 0DD, England
Tel. +44.87.0777.7202
Hong Kong Lifestyle Store:
Shop 1, G/F Guardian House
32 Oi Kwan Road
Morrison Hill, Hong Kong
Tel. +852.3106.3221
www.ligneroset.com

PHILIPPE COUDRAY
Decorative tapestries and chair upholstery.
6–8, villa des Nymphéas
75020 Paris
Tel. +33.1.40.31.02.95
www.atad.fr

PORCELANOSA
Tile, kitchen, and bath manufacturer.
Miami Showroom:
8700 N.W. 13th Terrace
Miami, FL 33172
Tel. +1.305.715.7153
London Showroom:
Wandsworth Bridge Road
London SW6 2TY
Tel. +44.87.0811.0345
Hong Kong Showroom:
Regent Building Material
Tel. +852.20.023.228
www.porcelanosagrupa.com

MASALLEDEBAIN.COM
*Solutions for your bathroom. Advice,
architectural counseling, and resurfacing.*
Tel. +33.8.20.82.18.01
www.masalledebain.com

ROBERT LE HÉROS
*Original furniture fabrics, curtains, and
trimmings.*
15, rue Tiquetonne
75002 Paris
Tel. +33.1.40.41.92.93
www.robertleheros.com

ROCHE-BOBOIS
Beds, sofas, chairs, coffee tables, shelves.
London:
421425 Finchley Road Hampstead
London NW3-6HJ
Tel. +44.20.7431.1411
New York:
200 Madison Avenue
New York, NY 10016
Tel. +1.212.889.0700
Beijing:
No. 5 Hall 1 Floor 008
No. 65, East Road at North Fourth
Ring Road
100101 Beijing
Tel. +86.10.8462.9033
www.roche-bobois.com

STENCIL-LIBRARY.COM
*Designer and manufacturer of decorative
stencils that can be used on a variety of
surfaces, including silk; an original catalogue
of more than 3,500 designs.*
The Stencil Library
Stocksfield Hall
Stocksfield, Northumberland
NE43 7TN, England
Tel. +44.16.6184.3984

S'TILES
A vast array of floor and wall tiles.
87–89, quai Panhard-et-Levassor
75013 Paris
Tel. +33.1.53.61.40.90

SENNELIER
*Painting materials with a large choice of
natural pigments.*
3, quai Voltaire
75007 Paris
Tel. +33.1.42.60.72.15
www.magasinsennelier.com.

TASSINARI & CHATEL.
*Refined and shimmering silk fabrics
reproducing designs dating from Louis XV
through the 19th century.*
Distributed by Lelièvre:
13, rue du Mail
75002 Paris
Tel. +33.1.43.16.88.00
www.lelievre.eu

TOULEMONDE BOCHART
*creation, design, and manufacture of
custom-made carpets and floor coverings,
coordinated textiles.*
10, rue du Mail
75002 Paris
Tel. +33.1.40.26 .68.83
www.toulemondebochart.fr

VOLT ET WATT
Lighting, swiveling wall lamps.
29, boulevard Raspail
75007 Paris
Tel. +33.1.45.48.29.62

WALLDESIGN
*Vinyl and textile-made adhesive creations and
creative wallpaper design graphics; possibility
of client-designed images.*
25, rue de la Forge Royale
75011 Paris
Tel. +33.1.43.48.30.24
www.walldesign.fr

ZOFIA ROSTAD
*Bright, contemporary, easy-maintenance
wallpaper.*
Tel. +33.3.22.46.87.00

BIBLIOGRAPHY

André, Jean-Louis, and Éric Morin. *Intérieur Extérieur, les architectes et leur maisons* (Interior Exterior: Architects and Their Homes). Paris: Éditions du Chêne, 1999.

Demachy, Jean. *Les Chambres* (Bedrooms). Les portfolios Elle deco. Paris: Éditions Filipacchi, 2001.

Dibie, Pascal. *Ethnologie de la chambre à coucher* (Ethnology of the Bedroom). Paris: Éditions Métailié, 2000.

Dougier, Laurence, Frédéric Couderc, and Deidi von Schaewen. Edited by Angelika Taschen. *Inside Africa.* Cologne: Taschen, 2004.

Les Habitudes de sommeil dans le monde (Sleep Habits around the World). Survey conducted in 27 countries on 5 continents by Isopublic, for IKEA Group.

Itten, Johannes. *The Art of Color: The Subjective Experience and Objective Rationale of Color.* Translated by Ernst van Haagen. Rev. ed. New York: John Wiley & Sons, 2004.

Laroze Catherine. "Songes d'une nuit d'été" (Dreams of a Summer Night). *A.D.* (December 2005–January 2006).

Leboulanger, Clémence. "Design & Sommeil" (Design & Sleep). *Maison & Objet* 12 (Spring–Summer 2007).

Malait, Marie-Jo. "Les bons génies de la deco" (The Good Geniuses of Interior Decoration). *Maison Française* (December 2006–January 2007).

Meubles de France. Paris: Éditions de l'Olympe, 1999.

Mirande, Yves. "Bedtime Story." *Maison & Objet* 12 (Spring–Summer 2007).

Sethi, Sunil, and Deidi Von Schaewen. *Indian Interiors.* Edited by Angelika Taschen. Cologne: Taschen, 2004.

Tiné, Caroline. *Chambres: Tous les goûts en 60 exemples* (Bedrooms of Every Taste in 60 Examples). Paris: Éditions Marie-Claire, 2004.

Ypma, Herbert. *Hip Hotels: Orient.* Rev. ed. New York: Thames & Hudson, 2005.

ACKNOWLEDGMENTS

I would like to give my warmest thanks to all of the owners who allowed me to photograph their homes and bedrooms during my many travels around the world over the years.

My deep gratitude goes to all of those who were so generous with their advice and assistance, particularly Rasil and Roman Basu, Colette Belle, Jean-Pascal Billaud, Marie-Claire Blankaert and Elle Décoration, Lesley Carstens, Christina Deliagre, Alan Donovan, Diane Dorran-Saeks, Christian Duc, Pauline and Luc Duponchelle, Louise Hennigs, Matheo Kries, Marie Lefort, Dominique Levy, Kiko Lopez, Marion Meyer, Hannes Myburgh, Aman Nath, Pia Pierre, Silvio Rech, Mirella Ricciardi, Philippe Seuilliet, Patwant Singh, Nathalia Struve, Angelika Taschen, Benedikt Taschen, Rosario Uranja, Mucky and Dieter Wachter, Francis Wacziarg, Meher Wilshaw – and many other friends who helped me to discover these magical and unimaginably beautiful places.

Thanks also to Laure Lamendin who opened the doors to Aubanel for me, Anne Serroy for her confidence in me, Francesca Torre for her insightful text, and Catherine Barluet and Julie Lecoeur for their beautiful book design. This collaboration was a pleasure.

DEIDI VON SCHAEWEN